MW01250728

MINOR HOCKEY TO NHL:
PARENTS SURVIVAL GUIDE

DR. PAUL M. VALLIANT

Trafford
PUBLISHING

Order this book online at www.trafford.com/07-1262
or email orders@trafford.com

Most Trafford titles are also available at major online book retailers.

© Copyright 2007 Paul Valliant.
Front and Back Cover Photographs Marjatta E. Asu
All rights reserved. No part of this publication may be reproduced, stored in a retrieval
system, or transmitted, in any form or by any means, electronic, mechanical, photocopying,
recording, or otherwise, without the written prior permission of the author.

Note for Librarians: A cataloguing record for this book is available from Library
and Archives Canada at www.collectionscanada.ca/amicus/index-e.html

Printed in Victoria, BC, Canada.

ISBN: 978-1-4251-3335-1

*We at Trafford believe that it is the responsibility of us all, as both individuals
and corporations, to make choices that are environmentally and socially sound.
You, in turn, are supporting this responsible conduct each time you purchase a
Trafford book, or make use of our publishing services. To find out how you are
helping, please visit www.trafford.com/responsiblepublishing.html*

*Our mission is to efficiently provide the world's finest, most comprehensive
book publishing service, enabling every author to experience success.
To find out how to publish your book, your way, and have it available
worldwide, visit us online at www.trafford.com/10510*

 www.trafford.com

North America & international
toll-free: 1 888 232 4444 (USA & Canada)
phone: 250 383 6864 ♦ fax: 250 383 6804 ♦ email: info@trafford.com

The United Kingdom & Europe
phone: +44 (0)1865 722 113 ♦ local rate: 0845 230 9601
facsimile: +44 (0)1865 722 868 ♦ email: info.uk@trafford.com

10 9 8 7 6 5 4 3 2

DEDICATION

To my children,
Kent and Nik for renewing my interest in Hockey;
and Mich for allowing me to appreciate other sports.

Minor Hockey To NHL: Parents Survival Guide

APPENDIX 3

ACKNOWLEDGEMENTS

Many people were inspirational while I wrote this book. To all the minor hockey players I encountered in my journey, I appreciate the memorable events that you have given me. Your enthusiasm on ice and motivation to play this game has entertained many. Hockey parents, including the good, the bad and the demanding have provided the scenarios which serve as examples in this book. I appreciate your courage to behave the way you have chosen in the arena. If all parents were quiet, reserved and non-judgemental there would be little to write about. Spectators who were at the arena to support the minor hockey players deserve special thanks for creating the atmosphere that every arena needs in this sporting event. The coaches who volunteer their time to teach children hockey skills, and the referees who prevent injury in the game deserve special gratitude. Stan Koren and Mike Heaphy deserve a special thanks for their evaluation and commentary. Last, to the researchers, columnists and sportscasters who have provided data for this book, I extend my gratitude.

FOREWORD

A great book, well written and to the point. Paul touches on many sensitive areas in his book. Having coached for over 30 years mostly at the AAA Midget Level; and a parent of a boy who came up through the Minor Hockey system in Northern Ontario, I enjoyed Paul's comments not only about parents but also about coaches.

As a coach, I have been very fortunate to have had the opportunity of attending a number of clinics and seminars over the years. These were meant to teach the coach ways of improving coaching skills. Experts were recruited to teach us drills for our goalies; techniques to structure our yearly plans for our teams; training and nutritional packages for our players. During my years of involvement in hockey, I never attended a seminar for parents.

In this book, Paul tells it like it is; the parent who hurts his/her child with their attitude. It is an unwritten rule in hockey "GOOD CHILD, BAD PARENT, CUT THE CHILD". Some coaches will take out revenge on a player because they have conflict with the parent. It makes you wonder sometimes who is the adult and who is the child.

I often wonder what happens on the thousands of rinks around the country when a bunch of kids get together to play a game of shinny hockey with no parents. They will make the teams, make the rules and play for hours. It seems the problem arises when we put adults in the stands, adults behind the bench, and adults officiating.

Paul is correct when he says very few players will make money playing hockey. I read somewhere, "THAT NOT ALL PLAYERS WHO PLAY HOCKEY WILL MAKE MONEY PLAYING HOCKEY, BUT ALL PLAYERS WHO PLAY HOCKEY CAN HAVE FUN".

- Mike S. Heaphy, Advanced 2 Coach
   1986-87, All Ontario AAA Midget Champions
   1992, World Hockey Challenge, Under 17 Champions
   1993-94, All Ontario AAA Midget All Ontario Champions

THE INFORMED HOCKEY PARENT

Minor hockey has always been about fun. This sport will get children out of the television and computer rooms and engaged in a physical activity. A youngster cannot assume a passive role in this sport. Once on ice, a hockey player is thrust into the game and becomes involved in a high energy sport. A player can only dodge the game by returning to the bench. From a practical point, playing hockey has many advantages which include physical conditioning, enhancing cardiovascular fitness and preventing obesity.

Hockey is a versatile and exciting game. It can be played in your driveway, on the road in front of your house, at an outdoor rink or at a community sportsplex. It is a simple game which requires complex skills. The rules are clear and in order to win, players on one team must score by shooting the puck into the opponent players' net. The main obstacle preventing a goal from happening is a goalie, whose task is to stop the puck. Hockey is a fast game which does not allow players much time to contemplate their actions. The game proceeds at a high tempo and a player's skills must be reflexive. Hockey players require the ability to skate and must have good hand-eye coordination. They should have the ability to "see the ice" and the reasoning skills to evaluate the play, in order to sink the puck in the net. The rules of this game have slightly changed since its inception date, but the general principles remain the same.

There are advantages to playing hockey. Kids who take part in this sport gain skills, discipline, friendships, team membership and knowledge of rules. Benefits for hockey parents include a healthy life style for children and friendships beyond the work environment. Enrolling a child in hockey will assist in their personal development. This includes building confidence, self-esteem and learning to cope with winning and defeat. Hockey introduces many interesting challenges for the child, but will create situations that are sometimes beyond the parent's control. This book will evaluate the many facets of minor hockey and provide the hockey parent with strategies to assist them in this sport. By having some awareness of these techniques, hockey parents will have the ability to cope with people and events that at times make minor hockey challenging.

The area of greatest concern in minor hockey appears to be the behavioral interactions in the arena. Aggression and violence in hockey have reached their pinnacle. A visit to an arena will show a display of aggression in its many forms. This includes spectators voicing angry remarks and players attempting purposeful injury on their opponents. Other examples include hockey parents yelling insults at players and at other times threatening referees with physical injury because of calls made during the games. The verbal abuse, threats, and physical fighting on ice have created much controversy for the game of hockey. At times these problems have been settled internally and at other times the police have had to attend games to maintain control in the arena. Crowds have had to be dispersed to reduce the prevailing mob activity.

During my involvement in hockey over the past decade, I have undertaken many roles in this sport. These positions as coach, trainer and hockey parent have provided me with some insight to minor hockey. This book will impart information that will assist in understanding your child's performance and interaction with players, coaches and referees. By reading this book, you will have a better understanding of human behaviour and the ways some people can affect your child's minor hockey experience. Techniques will be provided to assist in motivating your child to play this sport. Information garnered from this book will place you in the driver's seat and provide knowledge so that you can avoid situations that create frustration and disappointment. When emotionally charged situations do occur, you will have the strategies to overcome these personal dilemmas.

As a hockey parent, you will come to realize that minor hockey for your child is about exercise, cooperation with others and functioning as a member of a team. It is about developing friendships and skills, which can be used throughout your child's life. Minor hockey can assist the youngster in developing respect for others and building self-confidence. Some children will have the unique sensory-motor skills and the motivation to forge ahead in this sport and others will quit during their adolescent years. Not all kids are created to have the same level of talent in the hockey arena. Information will be offered to help the parent in understanding their child's personal dynamics in the game of hockey.

When I was first introduced to minor hockey, I had no idea of the decisions that went on behind the scenes nor the mechanisms used in planning hockey leagues. Over time, I became aware of the politics of hockey. The word "politics" is defined as practical wisdom, which can be prudent and expedient. As a hockey parent, I quickly learned that minor hockey created many behind the scene decisions which did not seem practical. Some of the decisions made by hockey associations seemed self-serving and seldom of benefit to the individual player. Furthermore, the decisions made by hockey associations and coaches were not always prudent. In certain cases these had an adverse impact on the hockey player and the hockey parent.

This book has been written to raise awareness of the many facets of minor hockey. It has also been prepared to provide parents with techniques that will assist in shaping their child, while they play hockey. By having these skills, the parent can equip themselves with some insight to this game and will have the strategies to provide advice to the child regarding acceptable practises on ice. Once the parent has completed this book, he or she should have better insight into minor hockey. This knowledge will provide the parent with a better way of evaluating the actions of coaches, referees, officials and other parents. Only the names of people who have appeared in public documents or public records have been included in the text of this book. Persons discussed as case examples in this book who resemble living or deceased people are purely coincidental.

Minor Hockey to NHL: Parents Survival Guide was written for parents. It is my intention to teach you strategies that will prepare you for this challenge. Minor hockey will present many enduring and memorable events. But from time to time, obstacles in this sport will create dilemmas. These situations can inundate the parent with conflict and force them to make decisions that are not always rational. By being proactive and forewarned you will be better prepared to implement decisions for your child and make your journey as a hockey parent a rewarding experience.

CHAPTER ONE

EVERY HOCKEY KID'S DREAM

Many kids on my son's hockey team have dreams about becoming NHL stars. When I've asked these minor hockey players about their chance of making it to the "big league", 90 percent of the kids believe they will become NHL players. What is even more interesting is that 90 percent of the hockey parents believe the same thing. There is nothing wrong with a child's dream of success in hockey, or his parent's dream, however there are a number of misconceptions about hockey that need to be examined. It is important for a parent to inspire a child's success in this sport, but at the same time the hockey parent must be realistic in evaluation of their child's skills.

Minor hockey players identify with NHL heroes because they have a dream about making it to the big league. This dream seems to be part of the hockey experience. Current NHL stars also had similar aspirations about making it to the "big league" and realized their dreams. According to Dan Diamond and his colleagues, 8,092 hockey players were drafted to the NHL between 1963 and 2003. The number of players who made a career in this sport however, was limited considering the number of eligible players over this 40 year period. Currently, there are approximately 900,000 players registered in Minor Hockey in North America. In Canada alone, there are approximately 600,000 players and the remaining 300,000 are registered with hockey associations throughout the USA.

A very small percentage of these players will make it to the big league and only the very talented will rise to stardom.

This book is about the survival skills a hockey parent will need in order to cope with the demands of minor hockey. The demands in this sport create undue pressure for the hockey kid and his parent. These start from the time a child commences hockey and extend into the later adolescent years, when a child reaches his/her pinnacle in hockey ability. Parents require strategies that will assist them in adjusting to the hockey experience. Assimilation of these strategies will make the experience enjoyable for parents and rewarding for the child. By having the survival skills, hockey parents can assist their child in making the best of their ability and adjusting to the demands of this sport.

Parents need to understand that minor hockey is an activity that can provide skill development and fun for the child. Some kids have the genetic talent to learn the advanced skills which will propel them toward success. Other children will struggle at each level of hockey development, but will have fun in this sport. Parents need to learn strategies so they can assist their child in acquiring the hockey skills. It is important however, that a child enjoy the game of hockey if he/she is going to perform well in this sport. Without an interest or desire for the sport, the child won't have the motivation to excel. During their early formative years, hockey is a recreational activity in which the child can have fun. Parents should encourage and reward the child for playing the game.

Parents need to realize that not every child is interested in playing hockey. Enrolling a kid in a sport that he or she doesn't enjoy will only lead to frustration for the child. Over time the child will lose interest in this activity. Children don't like to be forced to undertake activities they don't enjoy. Initially, they will accede to their parent's request because the youngster believes the parent knows what is best for him/her. With maturity, a child develops their own interests and will rebel against the parent for forcing them into activities they didn't like. Children must have some interest in a sport, and should have fun while they are involved in this undertaking. When children lose interest in an activity and involve themselves only because of external demands by the parent, this creates undue pressure on the child. Children understand the difference between fun and external pressure. Consequently, they quickly lose interest in activities that are labelled as "pressured sports". Some internal mechanism in their brain tells them that any sport which is not fun is not worth doing. Children who perceive hockey as having no merit will quickly lose interest in the sport and quit.

In North America, parents encourage their children to participate in sport. Some of the reasons for motivating their youngsters to undertake sport include physical fitness and prevention of obesity. Health researchers have demonstrated that obesity in children has doubled over the past 20 years. For example, Patricia Canning and her colleagues have noted from their research of preschool Canadian children, that 25.6% were overweight. Furthermore, Mark Tremblay and Douglas Willms have reported that from 1981 to 1996, rates of obesity in school aged children had risen from 15% (ie. boys and girls) to 35.4% for boys and 29.2% for girls. These researchers concluded that high levels of fat and carbohydrate intake, and limited recreational activity led to the burgeoning problem of obesity in youth.

It is of benefit for youngsters to be involved in sport. Exercise will assist in physical development and reduce weight gain in children. By encouraging your child to pursue the game of hockey or any other sport will emphasize the need for a recreational activity. This will reinforce the need for fitness and physical development. For the most part, children tend to be less active during the school year as they spend more time seated in the classroom. Seasonal changes in the northern hemisphere and a sedentary lifestyle influence the child to hunker down in their homes and watch television or play computer games. Encouraging children to venture outdoors or to a local community arena assists them in developing an exercise routine. A child who pursues hockey, whether it be at an outdoor rink or community arena, becomes involved in an activity which requires energy output, burning of calories and subsequent weight control.

There are other benefits to be found in hockey. This sport can assist in the development of skills. Furthermore, involvement in this activity leads to friendships for the child. A child's formative hockey development usually starts at age 5 and continues until the age of 17 when they attain their highest level of skill. During this period, they meet coaches and teammates who inspire and influence their skill development. Children meet many people in sporting activities who have an impact on them. Some of these people will create positive experiences and others will create negative experiences. The parent needs to be forewarned, and realize that not all hockey personnel will function in the best interest of the child's development. By having insight, the parent can quickly evaluate their situation and seek out options for their child when they encounter these negative experiences.

When children become involved in organized hockey, they pursue this activity because of the positive experiences they have during the game. Most kids will tell you they play hockey because they enjoy the sport and develop friendships with other teammates. Very few kids will tell you they play hockey because their parents force them into this activity. Fun seems to be the reason most children pursue minor hockey, and this alone seems to motivate them to continue with the sport. Players who don't find hockey satisfying will leave the game and pursue some other activity. Others who don't have potential, will play hockey recreationally well into their senior years because they enjoy the sport. A visit to arenas during later evening hours will attest to many old-timers engaged in the game of hockey. These players may not have had the skills to make it to the big league, but enjoy the game sufficiently to play the game during their senior years. These senior players, like many youngsters, have found some satisfaction in the game of hockey.

My involvement in hockey started at age 6 on frozen ponds in Northern Ontario. Most kids of my era were so eager to get out and play hockey, they would test the frozen ponds daily in late autumn to ensure the ice was ready for play. We didn't need much ice on the ponds;-just enough to support our body weight. Like every other kid of the 1950's there were the weekly pond and road hockey games and a gradual transition to organized hockey. Like many young hockey hopefuls, very few kids from my home town made it to the big league.

This book is about the role of the parent and the skills they will require to adjust to the demands of minor hockey. Many parents have journeyed into minor hockey with their children and have experienced the emotional demands of this sport. This book will provide some strategies so that parents can assist their child in adjusting to minor hockey. It is my intention to provide parents with knowledge that will make them aware of the unwritten rules of minor hockey. This will assist them in coping with the demands of this sport.

In minor hockey, there are many strategies that a parent will learn through trial and error. Many other strategies can be learned from coaches, friends and associates. Most of these will make the parent better equipped to understand the logical and not so logical decisions which arise in this sport. Involvement in minor hockey can lead to many positive experiences for the child. For example, the parent will spend much time with a child while they are transporting them to practises and games at local and out-of-town arenas. During these countless hours parents interact with their child. Hockey parents learn to appreciate their youngster's skills and can reinforce their children for their output.

Parents bond with their child as they assist the youngster in learning about the game of hockey. According to Erik Erikson, the bonding process is a stage of attachment which begins in the formative years of life. This process allows the child to develop trust of the parent and bonding assists in close identification with the parent. Being available during this stage of childhood and providing emotional and social support, assists with the child's psychological stability. According to Harry Harlow, children who do not have emotional support during the early formative years fail to develop emotional attachment and the ability to love others. Instead, these children develop erratic personality styles which lead to long lasting dilemmas in their personal relationships. Hockey is not the panacea for stable emotional development of the child, but a vehicle which can assist in good relationship building between the parent and the child. Sports bring parent and child into close contact and can enhance their social and emotional relationship.

Hockey is a sport that will establish objectives for the child. Parents must realize that enrolling their child in this sport will require a lengthy commitment on their part. Many children continue playing hockey well into their adolescence. Research supports the notion that youngsters require approximately 10 years of training to maximize their skills and to become adept at a sport. During this period the child spends much time with the parent, and a close relationship strengthens the parent-child bonding process. Kids need role models and parents serve as positive role models by encouraging their child's participation in sports. In time, the child learns to appreciate the parent's wisdom, guidance and advice. This interaction between parent and child further enhances the attachment process and leads to the development of self-worth in the child.

There are other psychological benefits to be gained from involvement in hockey which will assist in the child's later development. Jean Piaget, the father of child development, noted that children learn many skills in their formative years. Piaget's research has shown that a child advances through a series of stages from birth to adolescence. During this time, the child adapts their sensory and motor skills to the physical world around them. It is during this period, the parent can facilitate the child's development by encouraging physical activities which advance the child's sensory-motor skills. I remember the advice of a parent who told me a story of his technique for encouraging his son's hockey skills. Apparently, this parent made a small hockey stick for his son when the child was 18 months of age. The child frequently practised hitting a ball with his hockey stick while he played indoors. The child's parents praised him for this activity. As the child got older, his dexterity with the hockey stick increased because of his continued practise. According to the parent, the small hockey stick became an extension of the child's body. Daily practise with the hockey stick increased this child's sensory-motor skills and allowed him to develop good hand-eye coordination. This skill development continued throughout the child's formative years. Over time, the child's stick handling astounded the coaches. As he advanced through various hockey divisions, this boy's skills were noticed. During adolescence, at the age of 15, this young hockey player was drafted to the Ontario Hockey League.

During formative development, according to Jean Piaget, a

child proceeds through four sequential stages; sensory-motor, preoperational, concrete and formal. Physical, social and cognitive skills manifest themselves during this time. In the early stage, physical activity advances the child's sensory-motor and visual-spatial skills. The child learns during this period to coordinate motor and visual tasks. As the child proceeds to the preoperational stage which occurs between 2 and 6 years of age, the child learns to interact with others and reflect on everyday experiences. During this stage, the child learns to play and share with others and make simple decisions. Developmental psychologists acknowledge that the child's learning process during this stage allows for the development of cooperation and facilitates social interactional skills. By learning to share and cooperate, the child begins to understand the concept of "team work" which becomes necessary for later activity on the ice. Children who excel in this area will become good team players. Youngsters engaged in minor hockey utilize their social skills in cooperative interactions with others. With time this will assist them in developing and sustaining friendships.

In minor hockey, children must learn to pass the puck. They have to engage in cooperative play. They must also develop good sportsmanship and learn the skill of winning and losing. Situations arise in the hockey arena which are similar to experiences in later life. These can prepare the child and assist them in coping with everyday events. For example, many of the personal experiences which the child learns in the arena can be shared with team mates, friends and parents. The smile on the child's face as he or she learns a new skill can lead to confidence building for the child. The parent can use these special moments to praise the child for their accomplishments and to build self-worth in the child. After the practise or game, the parent can interact and bond with the child as they discuss the child's hockey experiences.

Children commence minor hockey at approximately age 5 and continue this sport until age 17. During this time, the child advances through stages of cognitive development. The child learns to reflect on their experiences, develop reasoning skills and learn the art of making decisions. At age 5, decisions are made quickly and without much thought. But as the child's brain matures, their ability to engage in complex decisions increase and problem solving becomes sophisticated. Parents can be influential during childhood and serve as a "sounding board" for a child's decision-making. The child's brain, being somewhat physically immature, does not allow him or her to fully comprehend information. For example, the "calls" made by hockey officials are not always clear. By being available, particularly during the concrete stage (6 to 12 years of age), the parent can assist the child in processing this information. Children and adolescents need input from the parent regardless of their intellectual ability because the brain does not fully mature until one is in their early twenties. Children cannot solve problems logically until they have matured. With their parent's advice, the child can carefully reflect on situations in hockey and this may prove advantageous to them in learning the game.

The hockey parent must equip themselves with many strategies so they can assist their child. Of special importance is the use of positive reinforcement (praise), which serves to build self-esteem and confidence. The parent who properly utilizes praise can highly influence their child's behaviour. The parent can assist the child by "shaping up behaviour" which will reinforce the child's skill development. At times in minor hockey, the parent will experience some tribulations and some insight will prepare the parent for these situations. Hockey, like any other sporting event, creates obstacles for the child and the parent. Examples of these are coaches who make negative comments about a young hockey player. Lack of diplomacy and hurtful comments can contribute to negative self-esteem of the child. The parent must be equipped with the skills to neutralize these negative comments. By discussing these situations with the child and aiding them in understanding these negative comments, the parent assists the child in coping and regaining self-worth. It is useful for the parent to have skills that will assist in re-building the child's self-esteem when spectators and coaches undermine a child's performance by their demeaning comments.

Situations will arise in minor hockey that need to be challenged. The parent who is equipped with some strategies would have the knowledge to address these issues. In conversation with the child, the parent can discuss these experiences and implement problem solving techniques. The events which occur on ice, in the dressing room, or in the arena, need to be explained to the child. The parent has to be ready to communicate and provide the child with a proper perspective of these events. Children need to understand they will encounter some people in the arena who express negative comments. The negative behaviours of some, is merely a reflection of a person's social and emotional problems and not a reflection of a child's behaviour. Children learn to process information, develop reasoning skills and evaluate the dynamics of behaviour. They learn the difference between positive and negative behaviour and learn ways of coping with those people who display deficiencies in social behaviour. The child learns not to take other people's opinions personally and to realize that talk is cheap. The hockey parent mentors a child in their reasoning skills. In time, children understand the difference between emotionally mature and emotionally immature people and learn to adapt to experiences while they are at the arena.

In minor hockey there are situations which will disrupt the

child's emotional development. It is at these times the parent has to be available to comfort the child. From the time a hockey parent's journey begins until it ends some 10-12 years later, parents will undergo many experiences. The parent must be adaptive in hockey and provide the best input to their children. An examination of libraries, book stores and web sites will provide the hockey parent with some information. These resources provide a plethora of data including techniques that can be implemented in a child's skill development. Some books provide testimonials from hockey players who have made it to the NHL. There are very few books however, which provide the parent with strategies they can implement to improve their child's adaptation to minor hockey. Furthermore, parents do not have access to the data that can assist them in understanding the unwritten rules of hockey. Some parents have never played this sport, and are only introduced to hockey because of their child's interest in playing the game. Parents do not have the information that will assist in their interactions with coaches, hockey associations, referees or other hockey parents. This book will provide the input needed to gain some insight into this fascinating sport.

When children first learn to skate, they struggle in their attempt to become proficient at this task. As time progresses, advanced skating skills develop in children who persevere in this activity. Children's interest in this sport will motivate them to higher expectancies and lead to the pursuit of organized hockey. Parents quickly find themselves involved with minor hockey because they transport the child to the practises and games. Many parents raised in the 21st century have never played hockey, nor have had any experience with this game. With time spent at the arena however, they come to realize the demands of hockey. Parents can benefit from strategies which make them aware of the guiding principles of this sport.

When children begin this sport, there is a sense that hockey is a positive activity. It is a versatile game which a child can play in the driveway at their home, or at an outdoor rink. Parents perceive hockey to be of some value because this sport motivates children to become involved in physical activity. Many hockey leagues espouse the notion that children who play hockey have little time to become involved in trouble. The motto, "keep a kid on ice and out of hot water" is a familiar dictum that many Hockey Associations support. Essentially, children who are involved in hockey do not have the time nor energy to engage in problematic activities. A child who plays hockey is busy with practises and games and has little interest in becoming involved in troublesome behaviour.

In my profession, I interact with some parents whose children have been involved with the criminal justice system. The process of attending Youth Court for a criminal charge is not only terrifying for the child but also embarrassing and emotionally draining for the parent. It is imperative that parents realize that by promoting sport and supporting their child's involvement in activity will utilize the child's time and energy and provide them with direction and purpose. An extracurricular activity will fill the child's spare time with an objective and a challenge. It will enable the child to meet new friends and have positive experiences. It is advantageous for the parent to support and encourage their child's involvement in hockey or other extracurricular activities. This is much better than spending money on legal counsel, when the child finds himself or herself involved with the criminal justice system.

Parents can learn strategies which enable them to avoid pitfalls in minor hockey. This sport can be a positive experience if proper preparation is undertaken. The advantages of hockey will certainly outweigh the disadvantages. Most hockey parents will admit that hindsight is the best teacher. Mistakes can be time consuming and have an emotional impact. By being proactive, parents can prepare themselves as they assist their children in gaining skills and adapting to the expectancies of minor hockey.

Most hockey parents have never undertaken a "parenting program" prior to raising children. However, they have done a competent job as parents. Some will admit that with added knowledge their task as parents could have been easier. These parents maintain they had no way of knowing whether they were responding properly to the demands of their role. Time however is the "master teacher" of all experiences. The positive outcome of life's events is the reward that one obtains because of their proper choices. With some insight, hockey parents can respond appropriately to the demands of minor hockey. They will learn that by responding to a situation impulsively based on "gut feelings" usually leads to negative consequences. Hockey parents need to engage in logically reasoned ideas which lead to wise decision-making in this sport.

There are many unwritten rules of hockey; however these aren't always spelled out for the novice hockey parent. Knowledge of these unwritten rules are needed by parents, prior to enrolling one's child in minor hockey. Without the best input, the hockey parent will not make sound decisions and this could have some negative impact on the child. For example, if someone were to ask you about the rules of being a hockey parent, you may not be able to provide an answer because you don't know the rules. Most hockey parents, have never consulted a "rule book on hockey parenting". A parent can only base their response on common sense, information received from other parents or facts found through research.

Hockey parents often follow the advice of other parents or learn strategies from their personal experiences. This approach however, will cause children to live with hardships, while parents seek a solution to a problem. There are many "rules" that become part of a minor hockey player's experience. For example, your kid's coach has expectations which should be discussed in the first hockey meeting. Without clear directives, the parent doesn't understand the expectancies of the coach. The coach may have a set of expectancies that are not always congruent with those of a Minor Hockey Association. Children should have fair ice-time but in reality this may depend on the coach's unwritten rules pertaining to ice-time. Furthermore, coaches have rules regarding benching of hockey players for infractions. The hockey parent has to develop some tolerance of the unwritten rules to ensure they can cope with the frustration they experience when these situations arise.

The way a parent responds to the demands of the hockey association and the coaches can have an impact on the child's minor hockey career. A good example of this can be found in the following scenario. My son and his teammate were having a discussion about an upcoming game. Some of my son's team members were injured and wouldn't play in an upcoming game. The coach had indicated that he would be selecting players from an affiliated team to take the place of the injured players. As the boys discussed their concerns, they wondered which hockey players would be selected from the younger Minor Bantam AAA team. One boy's name was immediately brought up as a contender for selection. My son remarked however, this player wouldn't likely be chosen because his dad had a difficult time getting along with others. The parent in question had a reputation for being unruly, loud, obnoxious and was not well liked by coaches or other parents. If this hockey dad had realized the impact of his behaviour on his son's selection in minor hockey, he may have changed his way of interacting with others. Needless to say, this parent's behaviour would have a long-lasting effect on his child's future selection on hockey teams.

Hockey parents must realize they need to interact congenially with others. In this way, they learn to fabricate positive relationships which support their child's involvement in the sport of hockey. Conformity to rules is beneficial in minor hockey because it is often a deciding factor on whether a child is selected by a team. Conformity is not only expected by the child who plays hockey, but also by the parent who supports and encourages the child's involvement in this sport. Hockey parents must learn the "unwritten rules" of hockey, otherwise their behaviour will have a lasting negative impact on their children. Coaches will not select minor hockey players onto their team, if their parents have a reputation for disruptive behaviour.

In the next chapter, I will summarize the "unwritten rules of minor hockey". Learning these guidelines will assist the hockey parent with an understanding of some of the rules necessary for adaptation to this sport. This is required so that a hockey parent can meet the expectations set forth by the coach. Involvement in minor hockey entails much interaction with others, before and after games. When parents don't get along with coaches or other parents, the hockey season can be lengthy, antagonistic and a drain on everyone's energy. It is imperative that a parent has insight regarding their behaviour and its impact on others. When negative behaviour is expressed in the arena, it can create problems for the child. Parents have to be aware of their personality style and its effect on others. If a parent experiences conflict, it is better to avoid personal contact so that problematic issues do not arise. A parent must always operate in the best interests of their child because to do otherwise can effect the child's hockey career. Parents don't have to like everyone they meet in the arena but should have the ability to cooperate with others and tolerate coaches and other parents on their child's team.

During the course of this book, I will provide the hockey parent with strategies that can assist them in adjusting to the demands of hockey. The techniques included in this book will enable the parent to better understand the impact of their behaviour on others in minor hockey. These strategies will exempt the parent from making costly mistakes that could jeopardize their child's career as hockey players. It is imperative that parents learn to display appropriate behaviour in this sport by learning to LEAD. This acronym would indicate that to become a good hockey parent one must learn to: (L)listen, (E)evaluate, (A)ask and (D)discuss. By engaging in these activities, a parent won't find themselves involved in offensive behaviour that will create hardships for themselves or their hockey child. By learning to LEAD, the hockey parent utilizes a realistic way of advancing the aspirations of their child enrolled in minor hockey.

Hockey has been Canada's winter passion for many years. It has become "the sport" of many kids who reside in the north. Hockey is a straight-forward game which requires complex skills. This sport is a multi-tasked activity which includes skating, stick handling, passing, checking and scoring on one's opponents. This combination of skills makes hockey one of the more complicated sports. It requires the player to have advanced sensory-motor, visual-spatial, body-kinesthetic and cognitive skills. Not every kid has the necessary tools to adapt to the demands of minor hockey. During competitive matches, one realizes the importance of the skills needed by hockey players to perform at a high level. Many children will acquire these skills and make it to Triple A hockey, but only a few will advance to Provincial, National, International or Olympic levels. Throughout this book, I will discuss the techniques the hockey parent can use to assist in shaping skills in their child. Some hockey kids will quickly adjust to hockey, whereas others will struggle and quit this sport. This book will teach parents the skills which empower them to cope with demands found in the Minor Hockey League.

CHAPTER TWO

THE UNWRITTEN RULES OF HOCKEY

Minor Hockey has many unwritten rules. From the time a kid is initiated into the world of hockey, there are guidelines that must be followed. These are dictated by organizations and enforced by coaches. The child who plays hockey and the parent who encourages this activity must abide by these rules. It is in the best interest of the hockey parent to become aware of guiding principles of minor hockey because lack of adherence to these rules may have some impact on a child's hockey experience.

If your child decides to join a hockey league, it is imperative that a parent becomes aware of the operational rules at the start of the season. Many hockey associations require the player and the parent to sign a contract of cooperation upon registration with a team. This binding contract implies that a child and hockey parent will agree to abide by team policy. The principles of fair play are provided by the team and supported by the hockey organization. Behind the hockey scene however, are many unwritten rules that aren't always discussed with the parent. These rules are enforced throughout the season and transgressions are dealt with by the coach. In the event problems escalate and become serious in nature, the impact can have a long-lasting effect on both the player and the parent. Conformity to team rules is expected and the coach will use a position of authority to maintain control.

The coach expects the child to adhere to team rules and also expects the parent will abide by these policies. Some of the techniques used by coaches to control a hockey parent are controversial but accepted practises. Coaches don't tell hockey parents how to act in the arena but will use techniques to ensure a parent's cooperation. For example, if the child does not arrive on time for the practises or games, the coach can't punish the parent. So instead, the child is punished for this infraction. Penalties for the player can range from pushups, laps around the ice-pad, missing a shift on ice or being benched (riding the pine) for the entire game. Inadvertently, it is at the coach's discretion to use punitive measures to control the activity of the hockey player when it is deemed problematic for the team. The hockey parent does not have any recourse other than to protest to the coach, who will respond by telling him or her to get the child to practices and games on time.

There are many ways that one can control another person's behaviour. In his book "Beyond Freedom and Dignity", psychologist B.F.Skinner maintained that undesirable behaviour is often controlled through techniques of negative reinforcement or punishment. In the world of minor hockey, consequences are forthcoming if the hockey player does not comply with rules. Hockey players are expected to be at practises and games on time. When they do not show up on time, coaches implement "learning models" to bring about the desired change in behaviour. By making the right response of getting to the practise on time, the child avoids the negative consequence of being benched. Many of the rules in hockey must be adhered to or certain consequences will prevail for the player. Generally, a coach will provide a warning to the player when infractions occur. By complying with these warnings, the hockey player avoids or escapes the negative consequences (ie. being benched, missing a shift on ice, missing a period of play). Coaches use consequences to enforce unacceptable behaviour. These include doing "pushups" or "extra laps" and serve as punishers to reduce lateness for practices or games. When players are punished for infractions, they are not given the chance of escaping or avoiding a penalty. In this situation the penalty is immediately delivered as a punitive measure. A child who insists on talking when the coach is explaining a drill, is told to "sit in the penalty box" (punisher). In this situation, there are no chances given for an infraction (talking) and the immediate consequence is time in the penalty box. Behavioural control is used as a means of enforcing the unwritten rules of hockey.

The coach does not have direct control over the hockey parent's behaviour but will impose corrective measures when the parent is perceived as not conforming to the "unwritten rules". For example, if the coach learns the parent is "bad mouthing" him, this can have some consequence for the child. To show their contempt, a coach will give the young hockey player fewer shifts on the ice, thereby aggravating and frustrating the parent. In the end, the child will pay the full price for the parent's transgressions. The coach is in a position of control and can make the hockey player's life miserable. The coach will sometimes act in a vexatious manner to demonstrate their control. The parent would be wise to retain opinions instead of sharing them with other parents, because negative statements inadvertently make their way back to the coach.

Hockey parents spend considerable time in the arena during their child's practises and games. With so much time on hand, they discuss many issues as a means of filling the time and avoiding boredom. Hockey parents like to interact and communicate with others about the latest happenings that are taking place on the team. A hockey parent's statements will sometime be taken out of context, and gossip will often filter back to the hockey staff. Coaches may become concerned with "rumour mongering", and parents who are labelled as "verbally out of control" will experience some negative consequences for their child and themselves. The impact will sometimes lead to direct confrontation by the coach. At other times, the hockey parent will receive a message indirectly as the coach makes his or her "unwritten rules known". In the latter case, the child will receive the brunt of the situation. One parent informed me that after complaining openly to others about her son's "limited ice time", her son received even fewer shifts. During this punitive action, the coach would look at her in the stands and smile. The message became clear to this hockey mom that the coach was getting back at her. It was the coach's way of saying don't question my decisions regarding your son's ice-time.

Hockey parents shouldn't give the coach a reason to punish their child. The coach controls all aspects of player activity on ice. This person has authority over hockey players and complaints will cause your child to bear the brunt of these situations. It is important that hockey parents don't openly criticize the coach. This behaviour always has a way of creating later grief for the hockey parent. The effect will not always be immediately experienced by yourself but it always has a way of catching up to you and results in a consequence for your child. Furthermore, hockey parents who openly criticize the coach usually suffer the long-term effects such as being stigmatized as a "rabble rouser". This type of stigmatization could follow the parent and the child throughout their minor hockey career.

In many ways, the unwritten rules become part of the team policy and over time the child and the parent become aware of these principles. The child may complain of these punitive measures, but in time begins to adhere to these as accepted practices. It is in the hockey parent's best interest to follow these guidelines and encourage the child to acquiesce to these rules. By openly complaining to the coach, the child and his parent will be labelled as "trouble makers". This negative status only creates later ramifications.

Becoming aware of these unwritten rules will assist the parent in adjusting to the demands of hockey. This will allow the parent to understand the impact of their behaviour on their kid's minor hockey career. By adhering to these rules, the hockey parent will make the best of their situation and lessen the burden on the child. Our society advocates "freedom of speech" which is guaranteed by our Charter of Rights and Freedom. Although most citizens believe in this principle, freedom of speech is not always guaranteed nor tolerated in the hockey arena. Hockey associations espouse written rules which must be adhered to so the Minor Hockey League can function in a legitimate way. The "unwritten rules" however, aren't clearly spelled out for the parent and it is only after an infraction that a hockey parent becomes aware of these principles. It is imperative the hockey parent gain insight to these guidelines. In this way the parent or the player will not have to bear the brunt of the residual effects delivered by the coach. The motto that should be adhered to by hockey parents is "be wise and don't compromise your child's involvement in this sport".

Many children commence minor hockey at approximately age 5. They will continue playing this sport until late adolescence. Skill limitations, physical stature, pubescence, motivation and other interests are factors that will lead to a child's decision to leave this sport. For a period of approximately 12 years, parents will have to endure the rules of hockey. If parents do not like the rules, they will carry a heavy burden for the period a child is involved in this sport. In this chapter, I will offer you some tips to make your sojourn into the world of minor hockey a little easier and trust that you will make proper choices to ensure a positive experience for yourself and your child.

Listed below, are some of the unwritten rules that I have learned over the last decade. Every hockey parent should have some awareness of these unwritten rules and utilize them. They will often be deciding factors on your child's ice-time, number of shifts and selection to elite teams. Transgressions by the parent could have long-lasting ramifications that will impact on them and on their child. Children who play hockey are sometimes stigmatized by their parent's behaviour. This negative stigma can follow the child for most of their minor hockey career. In this sport, hockey associations and coaches have considerable power and admonish those who do not comply with the rules. When the rules are not followed, there are punitive actions that follow. The sooner the hockey parent learns the rules, the easier the hockey experience will become for all parties involved in this sport. The following list is not rank ordered in terms of importance but merely a set of important guidelines that will assist in your hockey journey.

RULE # 1: NEVER FORCE A CHILD TO PLAY A SPORT THEY DON'T LIKE.

Children who don't like a sport will not play it well. Many parents ostensibly uphold the notion that children don't know what they like. This is true to a certain degree but is possibly only a reflection of the parent's perception. Children quickly come to appreciate their interests and abilities. When a parent enrols a child in a sport and the child does not respond favourably, the parent needs to re-evaluate their reasoning for this decision. Every kid does not like playing hockey. Children don't have the same interests. Awareness of this will allow the hockey parent some latitude in their decision-making. Parents may need to change their outlook regarding the needs of the child.

When I was a coach in minor hockey, some parents were impatient and frustrated with their child's lack of motivation to play hockey. These young players showed up for the practises and games but some were disinterested in the sport. They spent their time on the ice doing everything except attempting to learn hockey skills. Some parents were unwilling to accept the fact their kid did not like hockey. These parents continued bringing the child to the arena. This mindset created frustration for the young hockey players. Confused by their child's lack of interest, the parents asked what they could do to get their kids to participate. It was my impression these parents needed to engage in some introspection. They needed to appreciate the fact their kid did not like hockey. Lack of interest in this sport was obvious from the youngster's lack of activity when they were on the ice. A parent must consider alternatives when their child fails to show motivation toward a sport. There are many activities in the community which a parent can choose for their child, it is just a matter of finding the right one to suit the child's needs.

An interest in playing hockey appears to be reflected in the child's level of skill in the sport. Children who like a sport attempt to do it well. Those kids who don't like a sport show no motivation to do the activity. Others may like a sport, but never excel at it. This latter group of kids have the motivation but not the skills. They engage in the sport however, because of the enjoyment they receive from the activity. A parent cannot foster love of the game of hockey especially when the child does not like doing it. All the encouragement in the world, will not get your child to like a sport if the child has no interest. John Watson, a well known behaviourist once said "give me any child with reasonable intelligence and I will mould them into anything I want". As a psychologist I would disagree with John Watson's statement. Kids are unique and have an individual spirit. Neither a behaviourist, nor a parent can make a child do something they don't want to do. So, rather than force a child to play hockey, ask them if they would like to try the sport. After playing it for a short time, the child can make the decision to either continue or discontinue the activity. If the child voices an interest in another sport, whether it be a team or an individual activity, the parent should be willing to encourage the child's interest in this sport.

RULE # 2: KIDS SHOULD BE HAVING FUN WHILE PLAYING HOCKEY

Kids like to have fun; it is a measure of their identity as developing youngsters. Engagement in "fun activities" is something most kids would do all day if they were permitted. Kids like to spend time in activities and, when others are not available to join them, they often engage in solitary play. Many children perceive sport activities as stimulating and from their involvement learn to experience the rewards these situations provide. Kids often seek out activities that are fun and remove boredom from their lives.

Hockey is an activity in which a child learns skills; these include skating and puck-handling. These skills are practised frequently and after a number of seasons of play, the child becomes astute at these skills. Hockey parents evaluate their child's progress from season to season and move them to a level of competition consistent with their skill level. Hockey is a beneficial activity which offers fun and physical fitness. Parents want their kids engaged in this sport because it provides them with a structured activity. This facilitates and assists in developing skills and in achieving their goals. Some parents want their child to achieve big league status and view minor hockey as a step toward stardom. As I noted earlier, there isn't anything wrong with a parent's dream for their child. The hockey parent however, must be realistic and ensure the child has a similar aspiration for competitive hockey and the motivation that propels them toward NHL stardom. Otherwise, this underlying drive by the parent will create pressure on the child. A youngster does not have the reasoning skills to understand the need for long-term goals. Placing an emphasis on hockey when the child has no interest, and engaging the child in a pressured activity will remove fun from the game. The parent who consistently pressures the child to score goals, in order to create favourable statistics, places an extra burden on the child. NHL scouts are not at every game looking for potential candidates for the big league. By pressuring the child, the parent will only stifle the child's interest and motivation for the game of hockey.

The parent must maintain realistic goals while their child plays minor hockey. The youngster participates in this sport because they like the activity. Most children obtain some enjoyment from the game. The chances of a child making it to the big league however is not favourable. According to Jim Parcels, your child's chance of making it to play one game in the NHL is about 1 in 1,000. His research indicates that only about 1 in 5,000 hockey players remain in the NHL for a minimum of 400 games (ie. the approximate number of games that expand a five year period).

It is okay for the hockey parent to dream, because dreams motivate one to seek future goals. The hockey parent must be realistic in their evaluation of their child's achievements. The information that I have collected, showed that 90 percent of the hockey parents surveyed believed their child would make it to the NHL. There isn't anything wrong with a parent's dream for their child, but placing unnecessary pressure on your child will only create undue anxiety. By the time your child has reached his or her 16th birthday, he or she will have accomplished the pinnacle of their ability in hockey. If they have the skills, they will be sought out by scouts affiliated with provincial, state or NCAA hockey leagues. Some kids are drafted to advanced leagues by age 15 but only a few will make it to the NHL. Of those who are drafted and make it to the big league, there are few guarantees these hockey players will make it to competition at the NHL level. Dan Diamond and his colleagues have compiled some statistics in their book "Total NHL". According to their data, over a period of approximately 40 years, only 8,092 hockey players were selected to the NHL Amateur Draft. Of the players who made it to the NHL Draft during this 40 period, only approximately 45 percent played at the NHL level for 5 or more years; the other 55 percent were sent back to the minors or quit hockey.

The Hockey Hall of Fame was established in 1943 to honour outstanding people in the NHL. Dan Diamond and his colleagues have noted that from 1943 to 2003 only 227 players were inducted to the Hall of Fame. These statistics would indicate there are many good hockey players but very few outstanding stars. Not many players drafted to the NHL earn a permanent spot on a team and very few stay for a minimum of five years. These statistics should open the eyes of hockey parents who need to realize that minor hockey is not about making it to the big league but about fun and exercise. If the parent is realistic and believes these two fundamental activities are at the top of their list, they will never be disappointed by their child's success at this sport. If your child has natural hockey talent, motivation and connections in hockey however, the sky is the limit in this sport.

RULE # 3: PARENTS/COACHES SHOULD USE POSITIVE REINFORCEMENT

A child must show motivation in hockey if he/she is going to excel at this sport. Young kids don't always have the ability to set goals for themselves. Parents must keep in mind that kids between the ages of 7 and 12 function in the concrete operational stage of cognition. Their reasoning skills are not sophisticated as they process information. By structuring, encouraging and providing support, the hockey parent will assist the child in reaching their goals. Parents need to learn the use of positive reinforcers to shape the child's aspirations. Proper use of reinforcers will assist with a child's development. Parents who criticize, scold or embarrass the child, are not assisting a child but merely deflating and discouraging a child's performance. Quite often, negative reinforcement (ie.threat of loss of privileges) is used to motivate the child in the game. I have heard coaches who have threatened their players by stating they would not stop at a favourite fast food joint if the team lost their hockey game. This is a good example of the use of negative reinforcement because the child has to perform well in the game or face the loss of a privilege. Kids can best attain goals if positive reinforcement is used as a motivator. Properly delivered, positive reinforcers will increase the child's responses in the right direction. Hockey parents and coaches can assist the child in achieving their full potential but only through the proper use of positive reinforcement.

First year introductory psychology courses taught at the college and university level expand on the principles of learning theory. The behavioural model is at the root of learning theory. In his writings, B.F. Skinner stated that behaviour could be shaped through the use of reinforcers. Earlier, I discussed some of the principles of shaping behaviour. You will remember that positive reinforcers were noted as effective shaping

methods. Using a reward such as praise, following the completion of a hockey task, has a beneficial effect as it encourages
the behaviour and reinforces future responses. The parent who
encourages the child to do well in hockey by statements such
as "way to go Jimmy, nice pass", will reinforce the child's activity. This will create confidence and foster positive self-worth
in the child. The use of positive reinforcement will encourage
the child's output. It will serve as a reference for acceptable
behaviour and encourage the child in his future behaviour.
Positive remarks by the coach and the parent are essential to
skill and confidence building. Conversely, parents who emit
negative statements to the child, inadvertently decrease the
child's activity. Yelling negative remarks such as "what a stupid
pass" only creates negative self-worth in the child. The youngster who is given these negative remarks will be reluctant to
engage in future hockey activity (ie. passing the puck) because
of a fear of being criticized for making mistakes. Not passing
the puck serves to reinforce the child because this allows him
to avoid negative criticism from the parent or coach.

Activities in life are shaped by people who are important to
the child. These people include parents, teachers and coaches
who have an impact on a child's self-concept. People who are
in positions of authority in our society whether it be in the
classroom, or on the ice, need to be apprised of the best ways
to encourage behaviour. When I first became involved as a
coach and trainer in 1996, I was required to undertake the
Coach Level I and the Trainer Certification Programs. These
programs taught skills that would be needed to function effectively in our work with young hockey players. Coaches and
trainers were told not to use criticism. They were discour-
aged in their use of statements that would demean young
hockey players. These programs however, were never offered
to hockey parents nor did parents have to attend any training

sessions which taught the rudiments of "positive hockey parenting". In fact today, parents are only required to undertake a "Behavioural Program" if they are observed by referees making offensive remarks or gestures during a hockey game. In these instances, the "offending parents" are banned from the arenas until they are able to provide documentation to show they have undertaken this program. Parents are taught proper deportment while they are in the arena. The point that I raise here, is that parents involved in minor hockey should learn appropriate skills, so their behaviour doesn't impact negatively on hockey children. Only positive verbal behaviour should be emitted in the arena. This can best be summed up by the principle, "if you don't have anything nice to say while you are in the arena, then don't say anything".

RULE # 4: RESPECT THE COACH'S AUTHORITY

I recall the words of wisdom of a coach at the beginning of my son's hockey season. The coach had notified parents of a meeting to be held in a dressing room while the kids were on ice practising their skills. At this meeting, the coach provided us with his philosophy regarding hockey. His beliefs were reflected in the following statements: "There are two sets of rules if your kid plays on my team; 1) there are my rules, and 2) there are my rules. If you don't like my rules, you can take your child with you at the end of practise and don't come back." I watched as parents glanced nervously at one another and then back at the coach. Not one parent said a word nor questioned the coach's authority. Whether we were embarrassed, scared or humbled by his autocratic position, was not immediately known. Most of the parents in the room on that particular day wanted their kids on this coach's team because he had a reputation for teaching skills, creating teammanship and winning in competition. Rather than let his "words of wisdom" frighten us, the parents at the meeting decided to endorse their child's hockey registration card. Some parents would later leave the team because of conflict with the coach's autocratic style of leadership. By the end of the hockey season however, this particular coach would take his players to the Provincial Championship game and win the coveted trophy. This task would be accomplished with only thirteen players and two goalies.

The aforementioned coach had made an important point when he stated that only one person could be in charge of the team. In his mind, only the coach could be responsible for the decisions. He was making the point that in every organization, there can only be one boss. When too many people are in charge of decisions, confusion can frequently arise. Often times parents come to believe they know more than the coach. This assumption can lead to disastrous results for the team. Minor hockey coaches take on their role because they have more knowledge of hockey than most parents. Typically, the coach has taken a Level 1 Coaching Program, and some have played hockey at a higher level (Semi-Professional, Provincial, State, University or College). Coaches may not have great people skills and they may not have taken any psychology courses, but they generally have knowledge and an understanding of hockey.

Hockey parents shouldn't expect to be treated with "kid gloves" by every coach. It has often been stated that many coaches do not have good "hockey-side manners". So rather than worrying about the coach's social skills, attempt to understand the dynamics of good coaching and the skills they are teaching your child. Always keep in mind that most amateur coaches are not paid for their activities. These people are usually volunteers from your community. The coach may not interact well with people but is generally skilled at their role in teaching the skills of hockey. The best thing a parent can do is keep their opinion to themselves because no one has hired the parent for their opinion. Hockey parents provide transportation to the practises and games. They pay for the child's registration fees and purchase the equipment so their child can become proficient in the game of hockey. By expressing their disdain to the coach, only leads to consequences (ie. being benched, missing shifts, or serving penalties) for their child.

The bottom line is that coaches must have the control needed to direct a team. Hockey parents can't be involved in the decision making process. By signing the registration card at the beginning of the season, the parents agree to abide by the rules of the team. The child will usually pay consequences for the behaviour of the parent. So, as a hockey parent, don't aggravate the coach with your negative opinions (ie. bad mouthing or yelling). Every parent has to realize their child has a role on the team which includes performing as a team member. Hockey children don't need aggravation from the coach because of their parent's actions.

There are many examples in the media about parents who have difficulty in their interactions with others. Don't be the parent who makes the headlines in a local paper. It can be embarrassing for you as a member of the community, and will provide hardship for your child. Recently, a sportscaster affiliated with a national paper reported an episode of a hockey parent who had been involved in an altercation with the coach. Apparently, the parent was highly annoyed that his son had not been getting what he perceived to be fair ice-time. Supposedly, the parent did not like a decision made by a coach and decided to confront him. In the process, the coach was choked and others had to intercede to protect the coach. Police were summoned and the parent was charged with assault on the coach. Later, the parent had to appear in court to answer to the charge of assault. Although this is an extreme example of a negative reaction by a parent, it lends some credence to the fact that coaches are in a position of authority and they alone, have the right to make decisions regarding players. Sometimes parents don't like the coach's decisions, but must respect these to ensure proper functioning of the team. The parent may not like the coach's approach and does have the option of removing the child from the team. The parent can then attempt to find another team for their kid.

Hockey parents must show respect for the coach's position and must abide by guidelines. Parents sometimes have to swallow their pride and think about their opinions before expressing them. I can recall a mother who did not like the coach's decision to bench her son in an important game because the child wasn't performing at an acceptable level. At the beginning of the tournament, the coach had made it clear that he would do everything in his power to assist the boys in winning the tournament. He had stated, if he did not see the expected output during the game, the player would "ride the pine" for a few shifts until he was ready to deliver 100% effort. During the break, between second and third period, the aggrieved mother approached the coach in the hallway of the arena and expressed her discontent. The coach firmly mentioned that he would address her concern after the game. Following the game, he and the assistant coach met with the mother and informed her that if she did not like his rules, he would "release the child" from the team if that was her wish. He added however, that she should wait for at least 24 hours before making a final decision. After the game, the hockey parent discussed her concern with her son. Following the discussion, a decision was made by both parties. The child agreed to stay with the team and the mother agreed to refrain from her verbal abuse of the coach. The child believed that it was his coach's right to "bench him", because he was not playing at his level of ability.

There are times when a coach has to scold his players, so they will perform at their highest level of competency. It is at this time, hockey players have to become aware of their need for performance. Although the action of the coach can be embarrassing, it isn't intended to cause lasting emotional harm. Coaches from time to time will use every technique available to get the ultimate performance from their players. When this occurs, the parent should not take it personally that their child has been singled out. It is up to the hockey parent to adhere to the "24 hour rule" so they can cool down and take the time to re-evaluate the situation before approaching the coach on any hockey matter. Most hockey organizations espouse the 24 hour rule. They believe parents will come to realize their reactions are emotional and not based on rational decision-making.

I have administered "Anger Management Programs" to many diverse populations. These programs have been especially useful for those who have found themselves in conflict with the Criminal Justice System because of their assaultive behaviour. Anger management is not only beneficial to those who have conflict with the law, but also of benefit to those who find themselves easily frustrated by circumstances. The hockey mother that I mentioned in the previous example was emotionally upset because her son had to "ride the pine". Her emotional brain (hypothalamus) had become enraged by what she considered an unfair action toward her son. Her emotional reaction toward the coach was consistent with the need to protect her son. In her attempt to maintain some "motherly protection" she had become angry and responded aggressively toward the coach. William Cannon has noted that when people are angered or frightened, they express emotional behaviour. The notion of "fight or flight" is consistent with the hockey parent's need to aggress toward the coach. She was emotionally enraged and needed to express her feelings. By removing herself from the situation for a 24 hour period, would assist her in regaining some composure. This would allow her to cope with her emotions and reflect on her thoughts prior to discussing them with the coach. It is imperative that sound reasoning emerge when hockey parents find themselves embroiled in a frustrating circumstance. It is my opinion that hockey parents should be provided with Anger Management Programs when their children begin hockey. This is not because of their potential for aggression but as a strategy for learning ways of coping with their underlying feelings.

In the following example, I will provide you with a situation in which a hockey parent could have benefitted from an anger management program. In this particular case, a parent had noticed that her son received very little time on the ice over the duration of the game. This hockey mom openly berated the coach from the stands using some colourful expletives toward him. Rather than confront the mother in a public area, the coach ignored the emotionally distraught parent's tirade. After the game, the aggravated mother returned to her motel room because the team was at an out-of-town game. This hockey mom was not seen until sometime later that evening when she attended a social event for parents in an assigned "hospitality room" (ie. a room where one socializes, consumes soda, coffee or alcohol and commiserates with other parents about the events of the day). The aggrieved hockey mother did not abide with the 24 hour cooling down period. She was verbally aggressive toward the coach and threatened him by stating that she would not allow her son to ever play for his team again. Finally, in frustration and likely because of an alcohol induced state, she threw a beer bottle at the coach just missing his head. I was startled but not surprised by her action.

I informed a hockey parent who personally knew this lady to persuade her to return to her motel room. Having also experienced some problems with the coach, this hockey dad surprised me by stating "I'll hold the coach and she can hit him". I was surprised but not shocked at his response. He also had some underlying feelings of contempt for the coach because of past issues relating to his son.

The emotional reaction of anger is typical of people who are frustrated and do not have a way of displacing their anger. It is consistent with the Frustration-Aggression Psychological Theory espoused by John Dollard and his colleagues. They stated that people who are frustrated will generally aggress toward the object or person whom they believe to be the cause of their frustration. By actively expressing and engaging in aggression toward the coach, hockey parents believe they can resolve their frustration by venting their feelings. This reaction often occurs because people who are angered don't have the ability to quell their tempered emotions. Aggression is not the best way of responding to frustrating situations. Furthermore, alcohol consumption is known to disinhibit cognitive control and reduces one's ability to control their emotions. In lay person's terminology, this infers that when someone is extremely angry, they can not think clearly, nor do they have the ability to control their emotions. Alcohol has a dampening effect on the brain and interferes with the processing of information. When a person expresses their emotional feeling of anger, especially under the influence of alcohol, they are acting out their feelings. Contrary to what one believes, a person's reactions following the consumption of alcohol is "not the alcohol talking" but reflective of the person's internalized angry feelings. A hockey parent's internalized anger will make him or her do and say things which are not always consistent with their general way of behaving. When they are sober however, parents are capable of rational thought and have the ability to control their emotions and actions.

There are many examples of frustration-aggression in the hockey arena and these are becoming a concern for hockey kids and their parents. Often times, if parents are not happy with the coach's decisions, then they need to make an attempt to cope with this situation or seek out an alternate team for their kid. Luckily, the majority of hockey parents do not challenge the coach. They allow their kids to play hockey because they value the expert knowledge of the coach. They believe the coach's primary intention is to teach players skills that are needed in the game of hockey. Parents don't always like decisions that are made by coaches but they learn to "button their lips" because transgressions toward the coach will usually create hardships for the child.

Conflicts sometime arise between the hockey parent and coach. Some of these conflicts can be easily resolved within a 24 hour cooling-off period. By leaving the situation and thinking about their reactions, allows the hockey parent some time to cope with their emotions/feelings. It is during this time the hockey parent realizes that conflict is of minor importance. Parents realize children would rather play hockey than have their parents squabble with the coach. Generally, what emerges is a conflict of egos between the parent and the coach and nothing of benefit comes from these conflicts. As long as the hockey parent can cope with this "ego conflict" and swallow their pride, the conflictual situation can be easily diffused.

Social interactions often lead to conflict. Most parents can appreciate this in their everyday lives. Married people experience conflict in their relationships from time to time. A resolution of conflict requires a certain level of discourse, and there must be communication between parties in an attempt to resolve the underlying problems. Hockey is like a marriage, it creates situations in which negative feelings arise but need to be discussed. Rather than expressing negativism about some aspect of hockey politics, parents and coaches have to calm themselves so they can evaluate their emotions before expressing them. It is better to resolve angry feelings rather than express these directly toward the source of frustration. After a period of reflection, the conflict may become of lesser importance. Problems can be resolved when emotions are calm and thought processing rational. It is better for hockey parents to examine their reasons for emotional upset, talk these through with friends and attempt to resolve these in a non-offensive manner.

When people are upset, they seem to adopt a self-preservation response. This "fight or flight" mechanism tells the person they need to emotionally survive a situation. At times this emotional reaction can cause hockey parents to become upset because they can't cope with their anger. This emotional feeling of anger can sometimes lead to aggression as an externalized expression because the parent believes revenge is their only option. A hockey parent's contemptuous attitude toward a coach is based on the premise that an injustice has to be resolved. A number of behaviours, including verbally or physically attacking the coach, are sometimes used as a means of venting these feelings. At other times, the hockey parent may exhibit passive-aggressive behaviour. They will show their contempt toward the coach by their lateness for practises/ games, not paying fees when they are due, or bad-mouthing the coach. This form of passive-aggressive behaviour will not serve any useful purpose but only cause greater friction between the hockey parent and the coach. The direct impact will always be experienced by the hockey kid. Some coaches may attempt to obtain control of the situation by punishing the hockey child by not giving him or her ice-time. Conflict between parent and coach can leave residual effects on the child. Although these conflicts are sometimes resolved, they will be stored in the coach's unconscious mind, only later to "pop to the surface" and impact on a child's hockey activity.

Life is not fair and neither is hockey. I have watched and listened from the sideline as a spectator and a hockey parent. Comments are frequently made by parents and heard by others. Often times, hockey parents don't like the way the coach is instructing their kid and feel it is their role to provide feedback. This is a bad decision by hockey parents because most coaches don't want a parent's opinion. The coaching staff have taken on the responsibility of providing the skill training. So, rather than confronting the coach, it is better for the parent to step back and take charge of their emotions. This will allow the coaches to get their job done and make it easier on the child.

I remember an acquaintance telling me that his son had made it to the Ontario Hockey League. This talented adolescent was doing well in his play-making and goal-scoring ability. The player's dad became involved however in a heated discussion with the coach because he did not feel the coach was acting in the boy's best interest. You can guess the outcome of this scenario. The hockey player's ice-time dwindled and toward the end of the season, he was spending most of his time "riding the bench". The parent had good intentions but in his decision to provide feedback, had offended the coach. The young hockey player suffered the consequences of his dad's behaviour. The main point here is that parents should stay out of situations in which they lack knowledge and have no basis for expressing their opinions. The lesson learned is that if you want to have some control of the team, become a coach. It is of little importance to sit on the sidelines and criticize others. Hockey parents who criticize coaching staff will inadvertently create hardships for their kids.

Hockey parents come from a variety of professions. Status in the community, nor good intentions do not give the parent any credibility in providing input to the team. Your child may have exceptional hockey ability, but if you attempt to interfere with the coach's decisions regarding your child's time on the ice, this will only lead to problems. Remember, as a hockey parent your money only pays for team registration, equipment and transportation to the arenas. Your money or status in the community will not have any influence on the coach. If your child does not have talent on the ice, he may not be selected by the team. There will always be other kids with hockey parents to pay the bills. If you are not happy with the skills the coach is providing to your child, then it is time to find another team for your child.

I recall one parent who was agitated with his kid's hockey experience. In his mind, his child was the best hockey player on ice and was destined for the big league. He would constantly harangue the coaching staff to give his child more ice-time. When his attempts failed to have an impact on the coach he initiated harassment toward his child. This parent was often heard in the spectator stands yelling "you're not playing hard enough son, there are scouts watching you". His comments were especially embarrassing for his kid since his son was only 8 years of age. This hockey parent was unrealistic in his goals and by voicing his opinions, only increased pressure on his son. At age 11, the boy quit hockey and doesn't play today because of his father's absurd behaviour and demands.

Some coaches do not always have your child's best interests in mind. Whether you like it or not, some coaches only have the best interest in mind of a few players on their team. Those selected few who have hockey talent, are given more ice-time and more public recognition. Some coaches have a belief system which is biased and appears to be motivated by their own self-interests. Possibly, these coaches see greater rewards for themselves because players who excel will provide greater future payoffs for them. Some coaches are myopic and function with "tunnel vision". It is important for the parent not to waste their time attempting to challenge this type of hockey coach because it will only cause problems. The best thing that you can do as a parent, is to stay clear of this type of coach. In this way, your child will not have to bear the consequences.

RULE # 5: BE REALISTIC OF YOUR CHILD'S ABILITIES .

In the shadow of every good hockey player lives a great hockey parent. If your child decides to take up the challenge of becoming a hockey player, you will be busy attending to their needs. Being a good hockey parent means that you are going to have to go to extremes to provide for your child. The hockey parent learns quickly that they have to engage in a number of tasks; these include getting the child up for early morning practises/games, driving them to the arenas and shelling out the cash to pay for this very expensive sport. In the process, the parent has to provide the encouragement to the child when things are not going well. Parents must contend with the unfair tactics used by coaches, and verbal abuse from other parents. If your child is chosen to function on an "Elite Team", you will have to attend tournaments in distant cities. The toll of these demands on the parent's body, mind and spirit can be immense. Thus, before you decide to make a commitment in this sport, make sure that you have evaluated all variables. After the roller coaster ride begins, you can't get off until the train stops.

Most hockey parents with whom I have interacted have goals for their children. Essentially, parents want their children to do well in this sport and perform to the best of their ability on the ice. There isn't anything wrong with a parent's high level of aspiration for their child. But, at some point during your child's rise to stardom, you are going to have to remember that if your kid is going to make it to the big league, they will need the genetic talent, the skills and the motivation. Hockey parents must realize that most of these skills come from within the child. Every kid in minor hockey has some potential but it is difficult for anyone to predict the child's level of proficiency as they strive to excel in this sport. Coaches would agree that by the time a child reaches mid-adolescence, they have some notion of the child's talent. Young hockey players who excel in this sport are generally selected by "Elite Teams" or are contacted by hockey scouts. Some children peak early in hockey and show proficiency in their skills between the age of 8 to 12. The hockey parent must bear in mind however, that a child does not mature until late adolescence. It is at this time that the parent begins to realize the child's innate hockey potential. A parent must always remain positive about their child's progress and provide the encouragement. It is important to realize that by late adolescence a child will have demonstrated his or her true potential. By this time, the young hockey player will have exhibited the talent and motivation to excel to the big league because they will have reached their pinnacle of ability.

RULE # 6: ATTEMPT TO GET ALONG WITH OTHER PARENTS

Hockey parents are generally pleasant people. Some like to remain aloof but many like to mingle with other parents. It is best to display a congenial attitude because the hockey season is lengthy. To be in conflict with other parents, can only increase one's stress level. I recall my initial interactions with hockey parents when my child enrolled in the Tyke Development level. Most parents were socially interactive and pleasant people. These parents wanted their child involved in an activity that would provide exercise and friendships. The parents were not concerned about their child's skill level. As time went on and my son advanced to the Atom level however, it became obvious through conversations that many parents believed their child was headed for the "big league". Hockey parents would congregate before and after games and talk about their kids' talent and potential for the "NHL". Some parents would sit together comparing notes. On one occasion, I made the mistake of sitting in the section occupied by hockey parents from an opponent hockey team. Even though they were from the same town and I knew them from professional interactions in the community, I was asked by these parents "which team I was supporting". I informed them that I was at the game to enjoy the competition and the skills of the players. I'm not sure what they thought about my response. But, from that point forward, they watched with suspicion not completely understanding my reason for being in their "section of the stands". Initially, I felt as though I had violated some rule by invading a staked territory. As the game progressed, I watched in silence as the parents responded either positively or negatively to game plays. It was a good thing that my son's team lost on that particular day, otherwise I probably would have been mobbed for being in the wrong place at the wrong time.

In hockey games, opponents from either team aspire to rise to their highest level of expertise. Hockey parents need to realize this sport is about skills. Some parents perceive minor hockey as an activity where one is either a friend or a foe of the team. Much like the art of war where one is in an adversarial role, hockey parents seem to espouse the view "you are either with us or against us". This approach to hockey will only create conflict for the young player and his parents. Hockey parents need to take on a realistic perspective and attempt to show respect for children who play the game. Feedback needs to be provided regarding the "giftedness of the player". An unwritten rule of hockey seems to indicate that spectators have to throw their support behind one hockey team. The problem with this approach however, is that it doesn't encourage a positive approach toward hockey players but only encourages contempt for opponent players. I would advocate that it is best to refrain from making negative comments about minor hockey players because this approach only condones an adversarial role. Hockey parents don't always rejoice after a game, and some in fact take the outcome of the game seriously. If a child's team has lost the game, it can cause a long lasting effect on the parent's emotions.

Some researchers have found the mood in a community is greatly effected by an outcome of a hockey team's performance. The hockey parent whose child loses the game, may slink off to a distant corner of the arena to brood about the game. Research has shown this type of "sulking and grudge holding" tends to create stress. In fact, stress of this nature is known to raise levels of cortisone in the blood and leads to an increase in cholesterol levels and high blood pressure. Years of emotional upset can prove harmful to one's cardiovascular health. Some words of wisdom to hockey parents would be as follows; "enjoy hockey games and support players on the ice". Players in the Minor Hockey League provide much enjoyment to parents and spectators. They are not being paid for their on-ice activity and do not receive any rewards, other than the recognition given to them by the parents and the spectators.

RULE # 7: WATCH OUT FOR THE POLITICS OF HOCKEY

Hockey parents have to be on guard about their statements. If one insults or criticizes a hockey coach or organization it can have long-lasting effects. Parents who make offensive statements can have some impact on a kid's involvement in hockey. Earlier, I mentioned that hockey parents should avoid conflict with the coach. It is best to maintain one's distance or at least stay away from controversial remarks when it concerns coaching staff. It is also important to refrain from negative statements regarding hockey associations. These organizations maintain control of the hockey teams. The hockey associations advocate the rules and are responsible for the development of teams. People who sit at the administrative level of these associations, manage teams in a specific region and have control of the organizational operations. These associations will impose rules which strategically limit the movement of hockey kids from one region to the next. This is done to ensure that children with highly developed skills do not all migrate to one region thereby creating one strong team and many weak teams.

The rules advocated by hockey associations seem to adhere to the principle "for the good of all and not for one". Sometimes a parent will want their child affiliated with a team from a different region. Sometimes parents pursue meetings with association officials so their child is permitted to play with a team from a different region. This approach can sometimes cause "political backwash" and may disadvantage a child's future minor hockey career. To avoid "political fallout" from this type of activity, it is best to obtain a release from a hockey association. A hockey parent may want their child to affiliate with a certain team. The child who does not reside within the specified boundaries of the district however, may cause some concern for a hockey association. Some parents are successful in their bid to have their child relocated to another team but this process is time consuming. I can recall a situation in which a child had played for a specific hockey association but later wanted to play with a team under the direction of another association. The hockey parents had to pursue legal counsel in order to have their child released. The boy's father had to visit the Regional Hockey Association Office in order to have the case addressed. Following the hearing, the Hockey Association decided it was in the best interest of the boy to release him. I'm not sure whether it was the argument presented or the ramification of possible legal action, which led to the Hockey Association's decision.

Problems often arise when one challenges hockey associations. There is a high probability of ramifications from this undertaking. Issues of power and control become evident when conflict arises between the hockey parent and the hockey association. This sometimes has a way of backfiring and haunting a coach, parent or child. If administrative members of a hockey association believe they have been "challenged" they will likely hold grudges. The residual effect could be experienced by the parent later in the child's hockey career.

There will always be situations in which players don't get along with coaches and want to play for other teams. Minor hockey players will experience conflict when they attempt to get a release from a team. The general argument given is that the child's domicile falls under the direction of a particular hockey association. Often times, parents find themselves challenged by these situations. Instead of challenging hockey associations some parents purchase property in the district where their son wants to play hockey. With rights established by virtue of property acquisition and an address, hockey associations are reluctant to challenge the parent's registration of his kid in another district. Some hockey parents will go to extremes to ensure their child plays on a specific hockey team.

Sometimes there are repercussions for those who challenge hockey associations. Earlier I discussed the case of the father who had hired legal counsel to ensure his son was allowed to affiliate with a team in another district. The coach who had endorsed and supported this application also experienced some conflict from this situation. The following year, the coach applied for a position as head coach of a hockey team. He had many accomplishments in his career and had won many prestigious championships. This particular coach however was later blocked from taking over as head coach of a hockey team. The "politics of hockey" would indicate that one has to comply with rules. When rules are not followed these can have an impact on coaches, parents or players. Undoubtedly, collusion occurs within hockey associations and this can sometimes lead to decisions that are not always in everyone's best interests.

There are cases where the "politics of hockey" can have a negative impact on coaches and player selection. Young players and their parents can sometimes find themselves caught up in this process. A grudge may be held against the child, thereby preventing a child's later movement to another team. It is best to be wise in your choice of strategies for team selection so you don't find yourself in a compromising situation. Children deserve a chance to play on a team of their choice. Parents should have the opportunity to select a coach that will develop their child. Young players don't like to ride the bench because a coach does not like their level of talent. Kids know when it is their shift on the ice. They should not have to appease the coach just so they get their shift. It is in the best interest of players that "the politics of hockey" be given a back door so that youngsters can have fun and play the game without the political ramifications.

RULE # 8: QUIT ADVOCATING AGGRESSION AND VIOLENCE IN HOCKEY

Much to the dismay of parents, coaches and referees, physical contact has made its way into minor hockey. With body contact, aggression and violence have also prevailed. In Tyke Development, youngsters are not allowed to hit one another. A "danger zone" exists within 5 feet of the boards. In this area, youngsters are not permitted any physical contact with another player. This rule however, changes when a child reaches a higher level of hockey (ie. Minor Atom). It is believed that youngsters should experience physical contact in hockey so they can adapt to the rules of hitting. Hockey associations espouse that young players will learn to adjust to "body contact" which will reduce the possibility of injury. Recently, this notion has been shown to be inaccurate as medical researchers have found there is a high potential for head and spinal injury with body contact.

In higher level hockey, physical contact has always been espoused as a way of stopping opponents from scoring. It is believed that any player who encounters physical contact when they are attempting to score, will be cautious as they approach the net. This hesitation will cost them time and reduce their likelihood of scoring. Lingering in the hockey player's mind, is the "conditioned association" that any attempt at scoring a goal would result in physical contact which could lead to injury. From a psychological perspective, one can understand the impact of "conditioned associations". Ivan Pavlov, a Russian physiologist first made the discovery of conditioned associations in his laboratory experiments. Some years later, noted behaviourist John Watson, showed that fear could be instilled via the use of a classical conditioning model. In the game of hockey, "conditioning principles" are frequently in use. Whether one uses the Pavlovian principle of classical conditioning or the

Skinnerian principles of operant conditioning (ie. punishment), both serve as useful techniques to instill fear in opponent players. Aggression delivered by players will make the opponent players more hesitant to approach the goalie and take a shot.

Hockey players know that in order to win they must score on their opponent's net. To make this happen, a player has to be in the vicinity of the goalie. In the process of getting to the net, the player who is physically injured through aggressive contact is reluctant to complete a play. In the terminology of behaviourists, "fear" that becomes associated with being injured during an attempt at scoring will reduce the activity of the player. Deep in the unconscious mind, fear controls the action of the player. Hockey player's will hesitate for a split moment as they approach the goalie's net because of fear, and this will reduce their chance of scoring.

Many hockey parents advocate the use of aggression in the minor hockey. In the confines of the arena, one often hears verbal remarks including "hit him, take-the-body, cream him" as parental words of advice to minor hockey players. This prevailing mood has led to many acts of physical aggression on young hockey players. This notion seems consistent with the belief that aggression is a necessary ingredient to make this sport both challenging and exciting for the player and spectator. Often, youngsters are carried off the ice on stretchers because of the resultant concussions and body injuries. Aggression in big league hockey seemed to reach its pinnacle in the 1980's with hockey players signed to contracts because of their "enforcer qualities". NHL players were coached to engage in violent behaviour and rewarded with bonuses for physically injuring their opponents or taking key players to the penalty box with them. The principles of modelling have often been used to encourage children in minor hockey to imitate aggressive hockey heroes. This type of thinking in minor hockey however, only creates negative ramifications for the players.

Recently, aggression in hockey has undergone a transformation. With the implementation of the "new rules of body contact", referees have been given the mandate to reduce physical injury in the sport of hockey. Acts of aggression which have led to serious player injury have brought about a "new thinking" regarding violence in hockey. This new approach has initiated a change in hockey rules pertaining to physical contact. After a recent practise, my son returned home with a CD disk on the "new rules of physical contact". Ostensibly, Hockey Canada has developed a revised "Standard of Play Rules", to ensure the protection of kids who play hockey. The new rules that are enforced by referees will ensure that players are penalized for minor and major infractions committed during the game of hockey. Apparently, these newly expanded rules are necessary as safeguards in the protection of children who play the game of hockey. Hockey Canada advocates that children should not be engaged in aggressive behaviour during their games. A review of the New Standard of Play Rules indicates that players must not restrain, impede, hold, interfere, check from behind, slash, or cause checks to the head of an opponent player. Furthermore, players must show respect to other players or they will find themselves in the penally box for minor penalties, major penalties or game suspensions. These new rules of play should have beneficial consequences for the Minor Hockey League by advocating for a new style of hockey which will promote skills and play making in the arena. Minor hockey players will be expected to conform to these new demands and in turn hockey will become a sport which advocates "playing the game" as opposed to "destroying the player". Hockey parents will have to re-focus their spectatorship with the condoning of "smart play" as opposed to "aggressive play". This will reinforce the notion that hockey is an activity in which minor hockey players involve themselves in sportsmanship and respect of others in the fast game of hockey.

RULE # 9: ASSIST YOUR KID IN COPING WITH TRYOUTS.

Kids who play hockey have to learn ways of dealing with defeat. It is wise for the parent to be ready to listen to the child's concerns rather than expressing critical remarks. By emotionally supporting the child with encouragement and getting them to practise harder in an attempt to perfect their game, is better than criticising them for losing or not making a team. Rejection is one of the biggest problems that people face in life. Kids who experience rejection often have lowered self-esteem, become depressed and some contemplate suicide. So rather than placing pressure on the child, the parent must be supportive. Hockey parents must provide encouragement. They must be available to assist the child in coping with rejection or encouraging them to try out for other teams when they are "cut" by a team.

RULE # 10: DON'T CONSUME ALCOHOL BEFORE A GAME

This is a simple rule that serves in the interest of all participants in the game of hockey. In minor hockey, players shouldn't be consuming alcohol. Furthermore, it is not of benefit for the parent to imbibe alcohol before a game. Alcohol is a central nervous system depressant, which means that it depresses the ability of the brain to respond in a normal manner. Alcohol disinhibits one's thinking ability and causes a person to act in an impulsive and spurious manner with little regard for the consequences of their actions. Inebriated hockey parents respond in an uncensored manner when they are under the influence of alcohol. They will yell insults at referees, hockey players, coaches and spectators because the alcohol interferes with their ability to respond appropriately. In some instances, hockey parents will become assaultive. The behaviour exhibited while under the influence of alcohol is often a result of one's inability to censor underlying emotions (ie. anger regarding a bad call). At the brain level, ones thoughts and actions are impaired by alcohol. If the parent chooses to drink they should only consume alcohol after a game in a controlled and private setting (ie. home or motel room). Earlier, I discussed the example of the parent who lost control of her behaviour in the hospitality room. Even controlled and pleasant parents can exhibit raucous behaviour under certain conditions. Parents who have a need to consume alcohol should ensure their activity does not interfere with children who play hockey.

RULE # 11: HOCKEY IS AN ENDURING AND LIFE-LONG ACTIVITY

Hockey is a life-long-skill. Many kids will pursue this game into their senior years. When the parent conjures up the game of hockey, they should be focused on the long-term benefits of this sport. Many parents realize their kid's strengths and limitations. By the time a child is 16 years of age, innate talent, skills, interest and motivation will determine future aspirations. Rather than being annoyed with a child's decision to quit hockey, the parent should be aware of the accomplishments of the child. The hockey parent should attempt to acknowledge the child's personal development because of their involvement in hockey. Youngsters learn skills and gain fitness from the activity. The parent must remember that when a child quits organized hockey, they can always return to this activity in later life. Having the skating and hockey skills can be rewarding in many ways. People like to skate recreationally and will pursue this activity during their senior years. Skating assists with fitness and allows the senior to become engaged socially with other community members. Arenas offer public skating during the winter months when it is too cold in the northern hemisphere to venture outside for exercise. Moreover, there are many "old-timer hockey leagues" operating in communities and these promote fitness and development of friendships.

RULE # 12: DON'T VERBALLY ABUSE THE REFEREES

Referees undertake their position because they have a need to officiate at sports in the community. To become a referee one has to enrol in a program that teaches the rules of hockey. The payment for officiating at minor hockey games is about $15 for younger inexperienced referees and can increase to approximately $50 dollars for the more experienced referees. It is common in an arena to hear the crowd and in particular some parents yelling insults at the referee for their "calls". Sometimes this reaction is understandable because some referees make bad calls. Rather than creating havoc in the arena however, it would be wise for the parent to attempt an understanding of the call. Hockey parents aren't expected to like every call and should leave some margin of error for those who officiate in the game of minor hockey. If the parent believes the referee consistently makes biased or bad calls, they should put in a letter of complaint with the association which oversees the referees. Remember, that it is better to lodge a formal complaint in an assertively written letter than to assault a referee for his calls. The latter response will often lead to a court appearance and a possible criminal conviction.

CHAPTER THREE

THE ACTORS IN MINOR HOCKEY

"All the world is a stage
and every man and woman merely players"
(WILLIAM SHAKESPEARE,"AS YOU LIKE IT"—ACT 2, SCENE 7)

THE PARENTS:

I have met many parents in minor hockey. They come in different shapes and inner dynamics. Some hockey parents are pleasant and some are not so pleasant. Some hockey parents sacrifice their life savings so their children can enjoy hockey; they have no interest in reparation for their sacrifice. Other hockey parents expect their children will become NHL stars and return the money. Some parents define their sense of importance in the community by their children's success as minor hockey players. Other parents live in the humble shadows of their child's success. Hockey parents are an interesting group of people; they can be amusing, high spirited, aggressive and competitive. Some will make you angry and others will make you laugh.

Over the last decade, I have observed countless parents in the hockey arena. Watching quietly from the sideline, I have noticed them arguing with coaches, insulting referees and interacting with other parents. Some are noticed immediately by their boisterous and aggressive behaviour and leave an emotional impact. Others are calm and controlled and leave no residual trace of their paths. Last week I read in the paper about a father who was charged for assaulting his son's coach. He was unhappy with the amount of time his son was getting on the ice. His aggressive outburst led to an assault and he had to attend court to answer to the charge.

Parents play many roles in their journey in the minor hockey league. I recall many experiences over the past decade but one vivid experience sticks clearly in my mind. A coach had invited a group of parents to a meeting so that he could provide us with some information regarding the upcoming season. We were the lucky ones whose kids had just been chosen on a Double A team. Our children had been playing House League hockey for the last 3 years and were moving forward in their development. After much effort at the tryouts, the young players had been selected to move to the next level.

Walking into the dressing room, I observed the residual effects of what I can only refer to as "Tryout Anxiety". The Double A parents had been subjected to the cruel and usual punishment that comes with the hockey experience. The tryouts had been unforgiving to these innocent bystanders. The tension that had worn itself deep into the parent's facial muscles was beginning to fade. As they watched their kids on ice, the parents had experienced every move their kid had taken. From the sidelines, in quiet horror, parents had identified with their kids and felt every physical blow when they made contact with other players. An intimate but undefined bond had formed amongst those individuals who had assembled in the dressing room. Six sessions and nine hours of tryouts had brought this group together. While the young hockey players laboured on ice demonstrating their finest skills, the parents had fretted and worried. The emotions which had surfaced were now only beginning to fade into the parents' distant memory banks.

This was Minor Hockey at its best—kids labouring on ice to show their skills. These were the kids who could play the game better than their peers. They were the select few who had made it. Some kids had sailed through the drills whereas others had struggled to show their skills. The Double A coaches had set their standards high and only a small number of kids could clear the hurdle. Many hockey parents had departed from the arena with their kids in tow, disgruntled after only a few try-outs. They were disappointed because their kids had been cut early in the process. Some of these parents would later slip back into the arena to commiserate. By returning to the very place that had cut their hopes, these parents attempted to re-assure themselves the players remaining on the ice were worthy of selection. Some grumbling comments of discontent were uttered by these rejected few. The experience still smouldered in their shell-shocked demeanour, reminding me of the patients I had come to know from my clinical psychology practice. Like victims who had suffered post-traumatic stress disorder, these hockey parents conjured up the notion which psychologists define as "traumatized". Much like patients who had suffered emotional agony, these parents assumed a similar stupor. They could not come to terms with their child's inability to make the team. Rejection by the coaches had created much dismay and led to a loss of self-esteem for these parents.

As the dejected parents huddled at the edges of the rink they openly ruminated about their experience. Some expressed personal vengeance toward the coaches who had cut their child from the team. Their sense of shock and disbelief was evident as they discussed their plight. In the murmur of their whining, the phrase "politics of hockey" often surfaced like some brazen tactic used to strike down enemy on a remote battle field. These parents could only explain their child's poor performance with multiple excuses including fatigue, ill-fitting skates and bias by the coaches. In their moaning, it seemed as though some perverse calamity had led to their child's demise as a Double A star. This discourse of discontent would continue long after the tryouts had finished, only to resurrect itself periodically like some relic found in an archaeological dig.

The "tryout experience" had not been pleasant for many. Even the remaining parents, whose child had made it to the Double A team murmured their complaints in their quiet whines. In contrast to those parents whose kids had failed the test, the experience had left its paradoxical impact on the remaining few. The tryouts had been an uplifting but a humbling experience all in one breath. Reflecting back to the parents whose kids had not made the team was an experience of poised etiquette. It had been difficult to console them. These parents had been emotionally burnt by tryout rejection, and had a difficult time coping with the personal defeat. The hockey parent whose kid had made the team was wise to say nothing to them, but nod one's head demonstrating some quiet support for the emotionally injured. One of the best survival skills that can be learned as a hockey parent, would be the notion that it is better to say nothing than to provide an opinion to the emotionally wounded. Opinions can only lead to further trauma and negative ramifications.

The hockey parents who remained following the "tryouts", sat quietly in the dressing room breathing in the foul aroma left from the years of sweat and toil by minor hockey players. As minutes passed, the aversiveness of the odour seemed to decrease its attack on our nostrils. In quiet contemplation, I realized that many players had sat in this very same space, planning their rise to stardom. In contrast to the dampness of the arena, I wasn't certain whether this was a better place to be than the warm homes of the rejected and emotionally wounded parents. In my somewhat deluded state of mind, I came to believe the hockey parents whose kids hadn't made the Double A team were the lucky ones.

Very little banter surfaced in the dressing room as the parents waited for the coach to arrive. According to rumours, he was going to provide us with words of wisdom which would somehow enlighten our journey to the Double A experience. The hockey kids were now beginning to filter through the doors, their faces wet with perspiration. These young stars gasped deep breaths as they seated themselves on the painted wooden benches. They were the lucky ones, the kids who survived the "Tryouts" to endure their first practise on the Double A team. My son fidgeted with his helmet as he sat beside me. I reflected on the skills that he had learned over the previous seasons. He was a good skater and had mastered many of the skills needed in minor hockey. Even though he had started at age 6, he had quickly advanced his hockey skills.

Removing their helmets, the hands of the young players wiped the sweat from their faces in unison, almost like a rehearsed tactic practised on the ice. I could sense the emotional relief on the faces of these young hockey stars. Some of the parents displayed the same sense of elation exhibited by their kids. We had been at the tryouts from the start, eager and bleary eyed with our cups of steaming coffee. For many years, we had watched our young wards progress; now, these kids had reached the pinnacle of success. They had emerged on top and had just made their first Double A team.

A sense of apprehension surfaced on the faces of the hockey parents as the coaches filed into the room. The Head Coach positioned himself strategically in the room and nervously glanced at the "cow-eyed parents" straining to hear his words of wisdom.

"Hi, my name is Frank. I'm going to be coaching your child

this year. As you know, Double A Hockey parents have to be more committed than they were in Tyke development. I want your kid to learn new skills and will try my best to teach him these skills. Other members of coaching staff will be assisting with the training. The main focus we have, is to make sure that your kid learns to play hockey. They will be expected to work harder than they did in Tyke development. Fun and skill development will be the emphasis for these kids. We have the experience and can assist your child in improving his game. I hope that you will let the coaching staff do their job. Are there any questions?" he asked.

A sense of nervousness pervaded the room as parents glanced at one another. A few kids yawned audibly and one kid farted which brought some uncomfortable laughter for the parents, and smirks on the children's faces. Bill glanced over at me with a puzzled look. We all knew Bill very well. He was that hockey parent who sat in the bleachers screaming at the referees and cajoling the players. Somewhere in the vacuum of Bill's unconscious mind, he had wanted his kid to be successful in hockey. According to Bill, his kid was going all the way to the NHL. You've got to love parents like Bill, because they advocate the ultimate hope for their child. During Tyke development years, Bill was the parent who often screamed at his kid to skate harder and score goals. Bill was the guy in the stands who would often yell "the scouts are watching". He was the parent who believed his son's performance on the ice would somehow be noticed by "these invisible agents" who represented the NHL. Bill believed these agents from above would notice his child's outstanding talents and give him that telephone call which would ensure his kid's future stardom. Bill was his kid's best friend but, at times, could be every parent's worst enemy. Many parents had distanced themselves from Bill because they did not want to be tainted with the same brush. His loud and unruly behaviour in the stands created embarrassment for others. When his kid was on the ice, Bill was the menacing parent who needed to be avoided at all costs. He was every referee's worst nightmare. Occasionally, he was asked to leave the arena because of his aggressive offbeat comments. After the game, Bill was the parent who could be heard brow beating his son for not working hard enough and performing up to the "big league" standards.

As Bill stood up to present his views, the parents who knew him winced and retreated somewhere into their bodies. We had come to endure Bill's comments over the years. We wondered what question he would ask this time. In silent embarrassment, we wondered how the coach would respond to it. Bill stood up and barked out his question in an unapologetic manner.

"Coach who will decide on the amount of ice-time my kid gets? I know there are some kids who have been selected to this team because of their skills; but watching them over the last six sessions I know they don't all have the same ability that my kid has. I want to make sure that my kid will be on the ice to help his team win whenever he can".

For those parents who hadn't already been humbled, a sense of quiet embarrassment crept through the room. The kids on the benches showed some bewilderment. We all knew that Bill's kid was a skilled hockey player. His superb ability had lead to his selection on the Double A team. We felt some pity for this boy however, because Bill's expectations for his son were high. It was unfortunate for this kid that his dad did not have any social sense to recognize the implications of his complaints. Bill stood beside his kid somewhat perplexed and dumbfounded because the coach did not answer him immediately. We knew that in time, Bill's lack of hockey etiquette would inadvertently affect his son's career in minor hockey.

Bill had not learned to look beyond his own needs. He was convinced that his kid was bound for stardom, and through his rose coloured glasses was still wedged somewhere between reality and his delusional dream of stardom.

Bill's self-centred approach toward hockey is a good example of lack of common sense. Hockey parents should never underestimate the impact of their behaviour on others. The way a hockey parent presents to coaching staff, other parents or hockey players, can have some long-lasting harmful effects. By imposing absurd demands on others especially coaches, sets a standard for future evaluation. Humility is an important attribute and sensible hockey parents realize that coaches are not perfect. They select players whom they believe to have the skills to play on Double A teams. In minor hockey, some coaches may err in their selection of hockey players. As time goes on however, not all kids will excel at competitive hockey and they will not rise to the next level.

Negative comments made by parents are often noted by coaches. In their powerful positions, coaches control the selection of players. They are well connected in the hockey associations and will pass information to other coaches. Rumour is a very strong communicator which can create later conflict for your child. Offbeat comments inadvertently affect a child's progress in hockey and at times can have debilitating consequences. Parents who uphold views which are similar to those espoused by Bill distance coaches and strain relationships. They cause concern for coaches and parents connected to the sport of hockey. These types of parents, are the ones behind the scenes who advocate problematic behaviour. Their lack of thought, rumour mongering and general dissension, leave residual traces of stress on others. They play parent against parent and cause more havoc in the arena than one can imagine. Their passive-aggressive traits can be disruptive and impose chaos for others. Emotionally supporting hockey parents with negative attitudes only undermines the positive aspects of minor hockey.

Hockey parents are stressed. They are the ones who must get out of bed early in the morning to attend hockey practices. Traffic jams and aggressive drivers create further conflict for them as they attempt to get to the arena on time. There are a number of traits that will assist the parent and a compendium of personal survival skills the parent can develop. Being stressed out is not one of the traits that will serve any purpose. One must also remember that negativism has no place in hockey. This attitude can only lead to problems and create dilemma for the hockey parent. Negativism also creates harm for the child because others include the child in the parental package. Many youngsters are capable of playing high level hockey, but their parent's lack of social skills and common sense will create conflict for them. Impulsive comments create embarrassment, and rumours disseminated by others can have a long-lasting effect. A well-skilled hockey kid may not be selected to a team because of his parent's attitude. Hockey parents have to be wary of their behaviour and its impact on others. There is a time for expressing a view, and there is a time for retaining an opinion. Unless the comment is constructive and serves some purpose, it is best to keep the opinion to oneself.

Parents want their kids to play on Double A and Triple A teams. With this aspiration, the hockey parent will have to prepare themselves for a roller-coaster ride. Every kid who has the skills and the motivation to play hockey at a "select level", will be inspired to succeed. This will lead to much competition on the ice. Competitive hockey players usually strive to reach their highest attainable goals and only a few players will succeed. These situations will temper the emotions of the most steadfast child and create angst for the parent. The goals that minor hockey players strive for in life, have a price; this is the cost of Double A and Triple A hockey.

Once children have mastered the skills of hockey, they can attempt to advance to higher levels. Kids with hockey skills pursue their advancement toward elite teams. They attempt to display their competence in hockey so they can move forward. The child who possesses superior hockey skills including skating, passing, checking and scoring, will naturally move on to the next level. Every hockey parent has to realise that not all kids have the talent that will take them to higher level hockey found on Double A and Triple A teams. This will cause frustration for some parents but relief for other parents. There is a difference in skill level between Double A and Triple A teams. A higher tempo of play and greater motivation is often demonstrated by Triple A players. Kids on Triple A teams skate a little faster and pass the puck a little better than their Double A counterparts. Movement from the AA to AAA level will only happen if the child can demonstrate competence in advanced hockey skills.

Hockey parents must realize that every kid is not created equal. They don't have similar abilities. Parents sometimes come to realize their kid does not have natural hockey ability. They should never take this discovery personally. The child's outcome in hockey, should not reflect on the parent's self-esteem. A child's lack of ability in hockey is not a reflection on a parent's nurturing skills. Hockey parents by virtue of their effort should be rewarded for assisting their children in their attempt to adapt to the demands of minor hockey.

Many kids show a linear improvement in their performance until Peewee level (age 12 approximately). But as they proceed through adolescence their skills level out and they fade into oblivion. Other kids don't peak until adolescence and only become exceptional when their physical growth is complemented by hormonal changes. Cognitive skills proliferate because of the brain's neural growth in adolescence. During this period, sensory-motor functions are enhanced. Maturation of the cerebral cortex allows for the advancement of thinking and planning skills needed by young hockey players. Howard Gardner has noted from his research that people have different types of intelligence. Hockey players, for example, require specific types of intelligence including sensory-motor, visual-spatial and body-kinesthetic to perform well at this sport. The brain has unique internal structures that allow some hockey players certain advantages when they are on the ice.

The development of hockey skills is dependent on one's underlying genetics. These genetic traits will determine the youngster's adaptation at hockey skills. In its application to hockey players, sensory-motor, visual-spatial and body-kinesthetic intelligence assist in the skill development of the player. A child's inherent ability to display hockey skills will be determined by the physiological growth of the neurons in the areas of the brain that control these functions. For example, visual and motor skills which coordinate body movements, will enable the hockey player certain advantages. When these develop in unison, they enable the hockey player to "see the ice". This infers the child will have the ability to easily execute a hockey play because of his or her specialized abilities found in the cerebral cortex. The ability to "read the ice", creates a mindset which allows the young hockey player to excel at passing the puck or shooting at the net. These skills will lead to personal and physical efficiency on ice.

Every parent must understand that a child's hockey skills may fade as the child achieves adolescent status. The brain of the child is different from the brain of an adolescent. Some kids experience developmental lag as they age, which infers they may grow more slowly than others. On the other hand, some kids develop at an accelerated rate during childhood but fail to develop advanced physical skills during their adolescence. Hockey parents have to be perceptive of the skill-level differences in kids. Not recognizing this will only cause frustration for those parents who want their kids to become hockey stars. Some kids don't have the genetic talent nor the natural ability to excel at higher level hockey. Just because a child expresses an interest in hockey at a young age, doesn't mean he or she will have the ability to play this sport well, later in life. If the underlying brain mechanisms are lacking, a child may never become a skilled hockey player. As a hockey parent, you have to be aware of your child's genetic talent, so you do not get critical of yourself or your child when he or she is incapable of demonstrating advanced hockey skills. There are many kids who have a combination of cognitive, sensory-motor, visual-spatial and body-kinesthetic skills that will enhance their development as hockey stars. Conversely, there are many kids who don't have any of these unique features. When parents observe players on the ice, they notice kids with superb ability. These minor hockey players can read the ice, have good hands and can score goals. These are the type of skills which will enhance higher level performance in the game of hockey.

Hockey parents want their children to play upper-level hockey. They should, however get feedback from the coach regarding their child's skills. Parents tend to be biased in their perception of their child's ability. The coach however, will not have this same bias. If the child does not possess the skills, the parent can begin to recognize their child may not aspire to higher level hockey. The parent should understand that they need to seek ways of improving their child's skills. Through extra practise or specialized hockey schools, a child may get the final push needed to make it to higher level hockey. There is no guarantee that extra practise will assist players in learning advanced skills. Some sport researchers believe that hockey players require about 10 years of deliberate practice to become elite players. As I mentioned earlier, not all kids have the same natural hockey talent. It is in the child's best interest to undertake skill training to enhance their hockey performance. Parents have to be willing to encourage their children if they want them to progress to a competitive level. Spending the time and the money will ensure the child has the chance of acquiring the skills. With improved ability, a child may gain the confidence that could make him or her a better hockey player. The child requires ongoing evaluation to assist him in reaching his zenith.

Hockey parents should understand there are incremental steps as the child proceeds toward their goals. The parent must always remember that their goals are not always consistent with those of the child. Many kids decide to leave hockey in their early adolescence. A parent must realize that a child's decision to leave the game of hockey is their choice. Unmotivated hockey players don't do well at this sport. A child's decision to leave hockey should not create stress for the parent and this should not lead to a loss of self-esteem for the parent in the hockey community. Your child plays the game of hockey to suit their own interests and not that of the parent. Some parents get caught up in the process of hockey and often forget the true reason for their kid's involvement in this sport. Parents should not live their lives vicariously through that of their child. If the parent had aspirations of making it to the NHL, they should not impose similar standards on their child.

I recall a situation where a hockey dad bragged that all of his family members would attend his son's game because they wanted to emotionally support the child. This hockey dad described the experience as a family outing. He often encouraged his daughter to accompany the family to every game and tournament. Apparently, his young daughter did not express any discontent with this arrangement. During the hockey games however, she seemed distant and bored with her role as a spectator. Often she could be observed reading a book. As she got older this child did not participate in any activities. She had limited interests and no specific hobbies. This child's parents had expected her to emotionally support her brother but in the process had failed to allow her to develop an interest in her own extracurricular activity. When I asked this parent about his reasons for not encouraging his daughter to become involved in an activity, he responded that hockey was expensive and he could not afford activities for both children. Since his son had natural skills in hockey, he had decided to spend the money on his son. Furthermore, he added "I wanted to make the NHL but failed; I'm going to ensure that my kid makes it and will do everything in my power to get him there".

The expectations which parents attach to their kid's pursuit of hockey can create some conflict. Over the past decade, I have had the opportunity of watching minor hockey players compete for positions on teams. I remember one instance in which 13 goalies were competing for 2 positions on a AAA Major Peewee team. The players were challenged by the coaches at a number of skills to ensure they had the talent needed at this level of hockey. To the external observer, there was little difference in level of skill demonstrated by these athletic goalies. By the 6th tryout session however, only two goalies remained on the ice. The anxiety and tension experienced by the dejected goalies and their parents, was visible as they wept quietly and left the arena. One could only express some sympathy for the hockey players who didn't make the team. The parents of these rejected goalies also appeared despondent and depressed—rejection had effected them. It is difficult for hockey parents to detach themselves when their child is rejected by a team. However, they need to separate themselves from the process of "tryout selection/rejection" so they don't feel upset when their kid doesn't make the team. A hockey parent needs to have elevated self-worth, otherwise rejection from a team may be a debilitating personal experience.

A parent has to prepare the child for the best and the worst that arises in hockey, because all children who try out for a team are not likely to make it. Hockey players who are exceptionally gifted, will be noticed at the first tryout. The talented child will not have any difficulty making the team because the coach will immediately recognize their superior skills. The child who is competent at hockey but does not "shine" will likely have to attend more tryouts in order to convince the coach they are suitable for the team. A child who demonstrates particular skills whether it be at skating, shooting the puck, or checking an opponent could also be chosen to a team. Minor hockey players should attempt to impress their coaches. Players need to leave their mark early in the tryouts so the coach will not have any difficulty recognizing their skills over those of other players.

The hockey tryouts, whatever the level, will pose significant challenges for the parent. The process is lengthy and could last as long as two weeks. Daily tryouts will leave the hockey parent emotionally challenged. I have observed the anguish and impact of this emotional experience. The process can be stressful and taxing for the parent and child. After it is all over, the parent has to be supportive toward the child who doesn't make the team. A parent should not take the outcome of the hockey tryouts personally. A parent once stated, "how can I not take it personally?; my son was cut from the team!" It is acceptable for a parent to be angry about a coach's decision to cut their child from a team. It does become a concern, when the underlying anger develops into rage and this is leads to some aggressive act. Every parent will feel bad when the hockey tryout process leads to their child's rejection from a team. Rather than expressing their anger or resentment, the parent should assist the child in utilizing the anger as a mechanism to fuel one's energy. This will allow the child to work harder and perform the skills better when they try out for the next team. If this doesn't work out, then a better training regime may allow the youngster to excel at the tryouts the following year. There are many teams in the community and the parent can encourage the child to try and make it on another team.

Parents need to understand that their child may not have the special talent required to make a team. They should encourage the child to begin a conditioning program, which will better physically prepare him or her for the hockey season. Engaging in physical activities and making positive self-statements improves ones sense of well-being and gets the child prepared for further hockey development. Hockey parents should never allow their youngster to emotionally beat themselves up by engaging in negative self-statements including, "I'm no good and will never make it!" A parent should assist the child in reevaluating his or her skills and commence exercise and training programs to advance their skills. A youngster with limited hockey talent should never set goals that are beyond their level of achievement. This would only serve to cause frustration and could lead to emotional turmoil and depression.

The hockey parent must ensure the child evaluates his or her own skills. This allows the child to recognize weaknesses and determine which skills (ie. skating, puck handling, shooting or passing) need improvement. If a child is motivated to improve his or her ability, this can be undertaken through specialized hockey programs offered in the community. A parent has to realize that every kid does not have the inherent talent to play high level hockey. The parent can assist the child in recognizing and understanding their shortcomings. This will increase the child's awareness of their potential in this sport.

Some researchers have investigated parental attitudes and the impact on kids who play hockey. A recent study by David Bergin and Steven Habusta indicated that parents vary in their attitudes toward players. Some parents tend to be task-involved, whereas other parents appear to be ego-involved. Parents who are task-involved approach the game of hockey with a different perception than those parents who are ego-involved. Task-involved parents motivate their children to direct thoughts and behaviours toward improving their skill competence. Over the long-term, these task oriented parents assist their kids with personal achievements (eg. work hard in every practise so that you will acquire the skills to be a good team player). Conversely, the ego-involved parents focus on thoughts and behaviours that protect ego development. These parents attempt to nurture personal competence in the sport (eg. I want you to score a lot of goals so the coach will realize that you are a good player). Over the long term, the ego-focused parent loses sight of the real importance of the game. Utilizing an inflexible and rigid style with short-term gains (ie. points) does not allow the child mastery of the game. The ego-model of development, does not teach the child skills that will be of long-term benefit in improving their game.

Parents have to learn that it is best to foster skill-mastery and effort in a child's pursuit of sport. Hockey parents must be willing to listen to the child's perception of the game and motivate them in developing behaviour that will assist with their long-term objectives. Winning every game and scoring the most goals should not be the main focus of the game. In hockey games, one will see varied talent and some players will have superior skills. When parents or coaches only reinforce the "ego-focused approach", kids don't seem to do well in competition because the emphasis is not on team-work but individual performance. Hockey is not an individual sport and because of it's team emphasis, players need to learn to play as a unit. This can only be accomplished when all players have as their directive the mastery of the play.

How does one become an efficient and productive hockey parent? This is the question that every parent must reflect on. In order to convey the proper message to the child, parents have to be introspective as they interact with their child. The bossy, autocratic and critical parent does not provide positive direction to the child. In fact, this type of parent may only be encouraging unattainable goals. Most kids that I have met in minor hockey want to learn skills that will improve their activity on the ice. The parent's ideals cannot become the child's aspirations. Many parents have played hockey and have had their share of experiences in the arena. Some accomplished their goal by making it to the NHL; whereas others have played but did not make it to the big league. There are some parents who are still involved in "old-timer leagues" and continue to play on a regular basis. Hockey is a recreational activity and pursued in many different capacities. The point that I must emphasize here is that parents who have not achieved their personal goals in hockey should not impose their ego-ideals on their child. Kids who play hockey engage in this activity because they like the sport. They also play the game because they like to have fun. Imposing demands will only create conflict, ego-bruising and lack of fulfilment for both the parent and the child.

In minor hockey there have been many incidents of negative behaviour ranging from assault to homicide. Fortunately for players, assaultive behaviour is not the norm and homicide very rarely occurs. There are many forms of aggressive behaviour that emerge in hockey parents. In the following examples,

I will discuss some particularly interesting dynamics of emotions which will assist in an understanding of hockey parents. One would have to ask whether hockey parents are any different from parents involved in other sporting events. What are the underlying traits of hockey parents that cause them to become angry and display aggressive behaviour? I will attempt to answer this question by an evaluation of the nature versus nurture debate. This may assist the reader in an understanding of the mechanisms which propel hockey parents toward violence and gain them notoriety in the media.

The concept of "nature" explores one's biological traits and its impact on behaviour. Deep within the brain are physiological structures that control thought and emotion. Humans have frontal lobes in their brains which are responsible for decisions. These areas allow for the implementation of thought and action and inhibition of emotions. In some people however, there is a zone where emotions rage, and thought cannot control aggressive impulses. Some hockey parents are overwhelmed by their emotions when coaches make decisions which are not in their child's best interest. When these situations arise, some parents lose their ability to control emotions and feel the urge to aggress toward the source of their frustration. Like species of the animal kingdom who protect their young at all costs, the human species has the same preservation value. Buried deep in the emotional brain are the biological mechanisms that can cause a display of aggressive behaviour. According to I. Eibl-Eibesfeldt, the human species does not have the same built in "appeasement gestures" as those exhibited by the lower animal species. Threatened or defeated by their opponent, the lower species will cower. This serves as a stimulus for the aggressor to acknowledge dominance and leads to the cessation of the act of aggression. The human species however, does not appear to have the same underlying appeasement mechanism to inhibit aggression. Examples of this are sometimes seen in humans who will rage and continue an assault long after an opponent has been defeated.

In a later chapter, I will explore the underlying mechanisms of aggression in hockey parents. By the time the reader has completed the chapter they will come to understand that only a small minority of hockey parents have difficulty controlling their emotions. Most hockey parents will never be a threat to others in the arena whereas some will lose control of their emotions and express their feelings with rage. These are the hockey parents who are charged for assaultive acts and find themselves in court and in the media. Aggression is of little value when it is not harnessed and channelled into constructive energy.

Every event that culminates in violence has a starting point which initiated it. One has to ask what caused a situation to evolve and what allowed the underlying emotions to emerge? Why do some parents have the ability to control their emotions and others not have this control? Most aggressive underpinnings are generated from simple beginnings. Hockey parents are not a naturally aggressive group of bystanders who "snap" and exhibit homicidal behaviour. Sometimes there are situations which create frustration for hockey parents. It is in these circumstances that some lose control of their actions. Unable to channel these emotional episodes, the internalized pressure builds and leads to an aggressive reaction.

There is a fine line between control of emotions and the expression of aggression. Humans have a highly developed frontal brain which allows them to sanction impulsive action. There are a multitude of experiences that occur on a daily basis which activate a person's emotions. Some of these situations create internalized anger. But humans have a frontal brain and are able to challenge the emotion, and control their underlying feelings. When emotionally charged situations occur too often however, people tend to dwell on the situations that made them angry. This only creates more angry feelings and these situations fuel the emotion of anger. With time, anger can be transformed into aggression. Eventually, the person who experiences these emotions and is unable to block or channel these episodes, explodes into a violent rage.

Hockey parents are faced with many challenges in minor hockey. They experience stress because expectancies and demands by coaches create an underlying tension. When the tension is not properly diffused, some parents will explode with anger. Later, these same parents will question the mechanism responsible for their violent reaction. Finding themselves in court, facing criminal or civil litigation, hockey parents seem confused with their actions which led to a charge of assault. Most hockey parents don't appear to have premeditated intentions of assaulting others. Factors unknown to these hockey parents however, drive them over the edge and cause them to act in an abrasive manner.

An understanding of the precursors that lead to emotional reactivity allow parents to learn strategies that will assist them in resolving issues before they lead to a loss of control. There are many stressors in the hockey parent's life. Additively these combine, and over time can lead to a loss of control for the individual. It is imperative that hockey parents understand that reactivity is caused by underlying emotional factors which lead to a loss of control. An evaluation of these factors will allow one to learn ways of releasing emotional energy when it occurs. In this way the internalized energy slowly dissipates and does not create explosive reactions.

MINOR HOCKEY PLAYERS:

Talented hockey players are genetically superior. Their motor skills and ability to see the ice will make them better players than those without these inherent skills. The nurturing they receive from parents and coaches greatly enhance their personal attributes. A hockey player's ability to play as a team member however, is the key to one's potential to excel in the arena. I remember a great hockey coach once saying that "good chemistry is what makes a team work". In other words, players have to get along with one another so they can function as a team. It doesn't matter how skilled a player might be on ice, if that person can't function as part of a unit, the team will never excel on the ice. Hockey was never meant to be a one person sport. There are five players and one goalie out on the ice at the best of times. Hockey is a team sport and encourages group involvement at all times.

Hockey parents are aware of the concept of team-work because most are employed in a work setting with multiple employees. Parents recognize the importance of a cohesive unit in order to get the job done. It only takes one disruptive employee to create friction for the entire unit. The same principle applies in hockey and each player on the ice must function as part of the cohesive unit. In hockey, a child must demonstrate a set of skills that will get them selected to a team. In hockey tryouts however, the coach doesn't interview your child prior to selecting him for a team. One doesn't have to undergo any form of testing or respond to a personality questionnaire. The only real test is the child's demonstration of skills on the ice. The child must show the ability to perform the skills effectively with other members of a hockey team.

To be selected by a team, a child must always show his best performance in the first tryout. Research shows that when others evaluate performance, they do this in their first meeting. A child cannot wait for a later tryout to show their best level of output because by the second or later tryout it may be too late to impress evaluators. Coaches are like other evaluators of behaviour, they respond by selecting those who most impress them. This method of selection is known as the "primacy effect". This means the coach may have formed an impression of the child's abilities during the first session of the tryouts. Coaches don't have excessive time in which they can evaluate others. The way the player responds to the first session on the ice is used in the decision-making process. When the player does not demonstrate the essential skills, the coach has no option but to dismiss them from the tryouts. To delay a decision only prolongs the process of finding the best players for the team.

In minor hockey, a player has to demonstrate ongoing skills at all times. These skills are additive and increase with maturation of the player. A youngster's cerebral cortex is not completely developed until young adulthood. As the child's brain matures, the sensory-motor skills increase. A child will either become adept at certain skills or he or she will "peak out". Parents have to motivate their child to make the best of their skills. As mentioned earlier, the task-oriented parent attempts to foster mastery of skills which become useful for the child's hockey development. Children with natural hockey ability must be encouraged by their parents to perform at their greatest capacity. This will ultimately ensure their success in the sport of hockey.

Parents have to remember that performance is directly proportional to the child's genetic talent. Hockey players who have inherited the proper physiological constitution will possess the traits to develop advanced skills. Hockey players are unique and have innate skills and personality characteristics. These skills will make it easier to perform in this sport. Players who have the right genetic make-up have the "personal chemistry" to do well in hockey. A player must have the proper genetic talent before the coach can mould him or her into an effective member of a team.

Psychologists believe that genetics play a significant role in the development of characteristics. Some have advocated that in sport, genetics account for 50% of the variability for performance. This would indicate that one's genetic basis does have a significant impact on later skill development. Children who inherit genetic potential by way of their approximately 30,000 genes, could have the right combination of genes to make them superior athletes. These factors would provide the athlete with the right physical skills and personality to excel at a sport. Behavioural scientists advocate the other 50% of the individual's ability comes from learned factors including interest, practice, confidence, motivation, and incentives. In total, the combination of genetic factors (50%) and learned factors (50%) would cumulatively account for the 100% performance output on ice. Genetics essentially create the inherent physical traits (sensory-motor, visual-spatial, body-kinesthetic and cognitive processing skills) which equip the athlete to show superior performance. The genetic markers which influence physical skills combine with personality traits to allow for the later expression of these individual differences. Through practice, encouragement by parents and coaches, hockey kids learn to express their skills. These factors contribute to a child's ability to play the sport well.

Personality of the athlete is of some importance to individual make-up because it can greatly enhance performance. When a hockey team is comprised of too many tough-minded, opinionated, ego involved kids, this could represent a burden to the coach who must motivate all players toward cooperative teammanship. One cannot have too many "captains" on the same team. Hockey players need to recognize they will be treated in an equitable manner so they can function as a team. The leaders (ie. captain and assistant captains) have to be picked because of their ability to interact with teammates— they must have leadership skills. When a team player exhibits an "overbearing and pushy mannerism", it creates conflict for other hockey players.

Psychologists believe that individuals have unique personality differences. Gordon Allport has noted that every person possesses a number of specific traits. Those characteristics which he defines as surface traits act as the conduit for the underlying source traits. For example, an aggressive hockey player not only possesses characteristics consistent with aggression (source) but has surface traits which allow him to be competitive, tough-minded and achievement oriented. Furthermore, research by Theodore Millon has proposed that some individuals who possess negative personality traits can act aberrantly. This would imply that hockey players who possess traits consistent with passive-aggressive personality (negative trait) have underlying factors which cause them to show aggression (aberrant behaviour) toward others. Aggressive behaviour emerges in power struggles with team mates and with coaches. For example, a player on the hockey team who is not getting along with the coach will exhibit this passive-aggressive behaviour by engaging in specific behaviours (ie. not passing the puck or performing as a team member). These behaviours are done intentionally because of player's dissatisfaction with the team or the coach. Personal struggles that emerge on the team are often a function of the underlying conflict that members of a team have with one another.

Personality styles are unique in people. They are of little consequence to hockey players if the team is functioning well and winning games. In situations, where players have interpersonal conflict these personality styles can be problematic. They can create pandemonium for the team and lead to difficulties in performance. The impact of this is observed in situations of team conflict which arises when members don't get along with one another. If every hockey player is driven by their own personal and self-centered objectives, this can become disruptive to the common goal of the team. During hockey practises the coach serves as the figure head. The leadership skills of the coach allows for the smooth operation of the team. If one were to remove the coach from the ice, individual struggles would likely occur. Minor hockey players require leadership and directives. Hockey teams require the cooperation of all members in order to do well. Personality characteristics are not always evaluated adequately by coaches and should become of primary importance in the selection of team members.

When teams don't "work together", sport psychologists are sometimes consulted by coaches to analyze the factors responsible for lack of team cohesion. These specialists become an asset to the team because they can evaluate the dynamics of individual players. Coaches realize the importance of individual differences of their team players. Some believe the unique qualities of the players will allow them to be moulded into highly efficient members of a team. Hockey parents are aware of their child's personal characteristics because of the close contact they have had during the child's formative years. Parents realize that children vary in personality characteristics. A child may be tough-minded and resilient and capable of negative feedback (ie. scolding) whereas another child is emotionally traumatized by similar feedback. Hockey parents quickly learn to recognize their children's frailties and ensure the child is nurtured in a manner which is proper for their development.

The coach attempts to select a team with the notion players will function as a cooperative unit. Every child who decides to play on a team, whether it is House league, Double A or a Triple A league should be selected because of their hockey skills and his or her propensity to become a team player. If the coach knows that a child carries "emotional baggage" this could create problems for the team. These personal issues should be dealt with prior to signing the child to the team. Troublesome hockey kids can be a "thorn" for the coach and the team. Once a child is selected, that kid is with the team for the entire season. An entire season with a troublesome child can only become a problematic experience. In the event that a problematic child has good hockey skills and is deemed to be a positive team-member, further selection criteria should include an interview with the child and an interview with the parents. If the coach is still in a quandary regarding selection of the player, other criteria may be used including an attitude evaluation questionnaire or consultation with a sports psychologist.

There are many options for the coach when the hockey players are not performing as a team. The coach has to know the child and his/her perception of their role on the team. Second, the coach has to learn the parent's views because these could be undermining the position of the coach. Third, the coach must learn other team member's perceptions of the problematic player. The coach, assistant coach or sports psychologist (behaviour specialist) has to spend time learning the views of all players on a team. Once these points of view are understood, a team counselling session could be undertaken so these different perspectives are discussed. Group counselling has been used as a mechanism of understanding problematic behaviour and can serve as a vehicle of change. Sometimes, hockey players have concerns that must be discussed to enhance the proper functioning of a team. By sharing these views and getting some feedback in the group setting, the coach can understand and attempt to resolve the conflict amongst individual hockey players. The sports psychologist can serve as the unbiased observer to assist in rectifying these problems. There are ways of solving team problems and ways of creating team conflict. If the coach allows individual players to gripe, complain, or bad mouth other team players without resolving the issues this only creates further conflict. In this situation dissension prevails and the team fails to function well as a unit.

Human beings have a need to belong, a need for interaction, and a need for sharing ideas. Children grow, mature and become functioning members of society. Minor hockey is much like the social organizations that prevail in life. The challenges of teammanship and camaraderie that prevail in minor hockey will instill some of values needed to be productive community members. Children who learn to function well on a hockey team learn the fundamental behaviour of cooperation which is required in all facets of life.

THE SPECTATORS AND THE FANS:

Spectators and fans are interchangeable rolls. People who attend hockey games are there to cheer and support a team. These people provide the background music to the sporting event. Hockey parents must learn to appreciate the spectators/fans for their presence in the arena. They provide the enthusiasm and support to the hockey players. Without the spectators the hockey atmosphere would be absent. Hockey parents have a special challenge when they enter the arena. Since they are part of the arena crowd, they must show respect for players, coaches, officials and other parents. The hockey parent has to appreciate the dynamics of spectator behaviour in the arena because they set the prevailing mood during the game.

There are times when one does not agree with the "rowdiness" of spectators. By the end of the game however the spectators have to ensure their emotions are under control and not expressed toward others. What takes place in the arena must stay in the arena. Feelings of anger must not be taken to the parking lots or community. Being a good spectator would advocate the need to cheer one's team when great plays are made and goals are scored. Being a good fan also means to have the courage to recognize the importance of plays made by the opposing team. Showing a positive mood as a spectator brings a sense of fair spirit to the arena. Competitiveness is needed to charge the atmosphere and encourage the players during the game. Expressing positive thoughts toward the opponent players allows for a sense of fair play and an atmosphere which is conducive to good hockey.

Mob behaviour has been researched and debated by social psychologists. Philip Zimbardo noted that when large groups become hostile they undergo deindividuation. He defined this process as one in which social conditions (eg. atmosphere) produce changes in perception (eg. how we judge others) and thereby cause one to lower their threshold of normally restrained behaviour. Under these conditions, aggressive behaviour is expressed in violation of established norms. Once a set of emotions has been charged by the atmosphere of the arena, impulses that are usually inhibited by frontal brain control can be expressed in a negative manner (ie. yelling and criticizing referees). This leads to asocial actions, hostility and destructive behaviour by the crowd.

I recall attending a minor hockey game in which some parents were engaged in negative diatribe and making comments toward hockey players, parents, and officials. This situation of mob behaviour struck me with interest because I wondered about its origin and later asked the offensive parents why they had reacted with such contempt. Some parents told me they didn't have any particular reasons for acting verbally aggressive. They believed it was their role as spectators to act in a negative manner. Although the behaviour was tantamount to "deindividuation" as noted above by Philip Zimbardo, I also believed other psychological principles were at work allowing for "mob mentality and out of control behaviour". Research by psychologist John Dollard and his colleagues has shown that frustration often leads to aggression. Others including B.F.Skinner have noted that we are reinforced for our actions by others. Individuals who are part of a "mob" tend to reinforce and encourage one another to engage in aberrant behaviour. Furthermore, Albert Bandura and his colleagues have noted that humans learn behaviour through observation and imitation and are likely to act in a similar manner. Sometimes people exhibit behaviour that is not consistent with their general way of thinking. The responses that some people express are a result of their need to act in a manner they believe will lead to acceptance by the crowd. This serves to enhance expectations and create behaviour that isn't always consistent with one's personal views.

Hockey parents are often influenced by others in the arena. When they become aware that others are attempting to exert influential control, they must implement their free will and make a decision to refrain from unruly activity. Mob behaviour is not always consistent with one's personal belief system and quite contrary to the behaviour espoused by most responsible parents. Hockey parents who express prosocial and positive views become better spectator role models.

Parents can learn from their interpersonal interactions in the hockey arena. Spectators don't always like every call made by referees. However, most parents who attend minor hockey games have never taken any training in refereeing. Hockey parents have to realize that refereeing is a challenging endeavour. The outcome is dependent upon one's experience, observations and perceptions. Having an open-mind will allow the hockey parent to refrain from aggressive remarks toward referees, which goes against the grain of fair-play in the arena.

THE REFEREES: THEIR IMPACT ON PARENTS AND PLAYERS.

I first started watching NHL hockey in 1957. At that time I understood the role of the referee as one which gave them the power to make calls. I am a believer in rules in hockey as they set the tone for fair-play during a game. Without rules in any game, anarchy would prevail and the outcome would be left to the discretion of the players. Some of the earliest hockey games in which I played did not have any referees invoking the rules of hockey. For the most part these games flowed smoothly because all players had agreed on a set of rules at the start of the game. Most kids who participated had a rudimentary understanding of the rules from their personal experience watching NHL hockey on Saturday evenings.

Referees are either loved or hated. They can make your day at the arena or destroy it. They are in control of the game or out of control. What makes the job of referee such an arduous task? Being the judge of someone's behaviour places one in a difficult position. Fair-play is advocated for those who officiate at games and rules of conduct are laid out in certification programs for coaches and trainers. Referees are expected to undertake training in officiating and follow guidelines mandated by their organization. There are different motivations for becoming a referee in Minor Hockey and a variety of refereeing styles. An overview of this area will allow the hockey parent an understanding of the complex role of the referee.

The atmosphere of the hockey game is often reflective of the calls made by referees. These officials are often evaluated according to the way they conduct themselves during the game.

Consider the role of the referee in the game of hockey. This person has expert knowledge of the rules of hockey. The referee controls the activities of players, coaches, and spectators during the game. To be placed in this position requires courage at best, because the referee is in the spotlight and must be responsible for every decision that is made during the game. The referee's decisions will bring about a number of reactions from highly charged players, coaches and fans. Hockey is a sport with high tempo and decisions made by the referee have to be made quickly. Often times these are made reflexively and at other times the referee must consult with the linesmen, to ensure the decision is a good call. According to Pierre Trudel and his colleagues, referees are observant of on-ice behaviour in minor hockey and spend 44.7% of their game monitoring the play without any interaction; 40.6% intervening with gestures or verbal interaction; and 13% of the game waiting and observing the behaviour of players.

The game of hockey has a standard protocol when it comes to regulations. At times referees can make calls that create an emotional fervour in the arena. Players will react with disdain, fans and spectators voice their disapproval, and a negative mood can prevail. There are some concerns expressed by fans when referees make decisions quickly, especially when these do not favour one's team. These "biased calls" appear to be based upon the perception of the referee at the time of the infraction. Research has shown that many variables interfere with the referee's perception of events. These include the lighting, visual observations, location of the incident, prior occurrences, and the mood of the fans. The referee's call is also a function of other variables which include past experience and knowledge of the rules. Personal factors including physical, emotional, and mental condition of the referee can also influence their behaviour. Furthermore, cognitive factors including reasoning and analytical ability will influence the decisions of the referees. The perceptual ability to judge a situation will lead to varied opinions because no two people react in the same manner to a situation. Having sound knowledge of the game of hockey and its rules, assists the referee in making good calls. Hockey Canada has recently changed many of the rules of hockey in response to the aggressive acts that were causing injury to players. Referees have had to return to school to re-learn some of the guiding principles of hockey (ie. New Standards of Play). Knowledge of these rules lead to their responses during the game.

Often times a call made by the referee will lead to frustration by those in attendance at the game. The spectators must practise coping skills in order to deal with these calls. Fans in the crowd can become aggressive and incite much anger when a call seems inappropriate. The spectator must attempt to adhere to the principles of fair-play. Parents need to be supportive of the referee's call and should not question his judgement in public. If one is concerned about consistent bad calls, the spectator should make a complaint with the association responsible for regulating the referees. Some referees have indicated that, at times they feel verbally and emotionally abused by spectators who scream out negative comments at them after making a call. One of the first principles of fairness should be to say nothing if the spectator doesn't like the call. Rather than screaming at the referee (ie."are you stupid making that call ref"), spectators should condone good calls by voicing a positive opinion (ie."good call ref"). This will reinforce the referee for their observant behaviour and condone good calls. By protecting the rights of the players, the referees are doing their job and ensuring that injury does not occur to players. Parents must remember their child is on the ice, and when referees don't do their job this could lead to serious injury for players.

Parents don't want their children injured in hockey, so it is in their best interest to watch the game and not interfere with the referee's role. No one likes others who tell them how to do their job. When hockey parents emotionally voice their disdain for a call, this only creates emotional havoc for the referee.

Amateur referees who officiate at games are not paid much for their game expertise. Apparently they receive approximately $15 to $50 per game depending upon their qualifications and experience. These officials are under pressure as they attempt to watch every hockey play with scrutiny. The abuse waged toward the referees is exacerbated by spectators who are often heard cajoling the referee for a call. It would appear the referee is the most despised person in the arena. The spectators somehow believe the referees should be expected to take the abuse because it is commensurate with their role as an official. In response to the abusiveness toward referees, many hockey associations have imposed sanctions by dispersing fans from the arena for their offensive language or gestures.

There are many examples of the abuse toward referees. These overt acts can be observed at minor hockey games. Recently, I witnessed an example of this type of behaviour. Two Midget AAA hockey teams were engaged in a regular season game. One team was in first place and the other in fourth place as the season was nearing completion. The fourth place team was known for their solid but aggressive game, whereas the first place team consisted of younger but highly skilled players. The referee was aware of the rivalry between these teams. He had officiated at many of their games and was now in this precarious position once again. At the commencement of the game, the referee cautioned the hockey players from both teams that he would not condone aggressive behaviour.

Many penalty calls were made in the first period and the hockey players soon realized the referee would not tolerate any transgressions. During the second period it was obvious to spectators that many of the players were attempting to conform to the rules of play. By the end of the second period, the first place team was out-performing the fourth place team. The frustration was evident in some players. Altercations on the ice occurred frequently and the penalty boxes started filling up with disgruntled players. In one instance, a hockey player had exceeded his limit in penalties and was expelled from the game. As the player left the ice, some spectators cheered the hockey player's expulsion. In response, the player gave the spectators an index finger salute. The referee was quick to recognize the infraction and gave the player an automatic one game suspension for unsportsman-like conduct.

During the third period, aggressive behaviour once again led to many penalties. One parent, having become upset with a call, hurled verbal insults at the referee. The parent was clearly out of control and the referee disparaged by the parent's remarks quickly responded, telling the offensive father to leave the arena. Highly emotionally aroused by this time, the banned father yelled more negative remarks at the referee as he begrudgingly left the rink. By his actions, the referee demonstrated that he was in charge of the game. He had maintained control of the game and had not tolerated offensive player or spectator behaviour.

Some hockey parents continued to display offensive behaviour with their verbal insults toward the referee but these were kept at a low monotone and were not heard by the referee. The spectators had learned from the referee's actions, that he would banish those who created problems in the arena. His calls allowed the spectators and the players to acknowledge his expert opinion and respect his officiating. The spectators conceded to the officiating because they understood that sanctions would be given in response to transgressions. By the end of the game, it was evident the referee and linesmen had done a remarkably good job at controlling the mood in the arena.

Following the game, the referee left the ice with his two linesmen and walked toward the dressing room used by the officials. The hockey parent who had been told to leave the arena was in the lobby waiting for his son. When he saw the referee he verbalized his feelings regarding the game and made some offensive remarks. In response, the referee removed his helmet and sweater and gestured to the abusive hockey parent "here you might as well put these on and referee the next game because you seem to know more about it than I do". Those standing in the lobby had expected a physical altercation but instead witnessed a referee who was very much in control of his emotions. He had acted assertively in his response to the offensive parent. This official could have chosen a variety of responses from saying nothing to physically attacking the parent. Instead he chose to make a comment which led to embarrassment for the parent. This was an admirable response of a seasoned referee who had learned to control not only his emotions but also the emotions of the crowd.

Many parents witnessed the incident and immediately informed the offensive parent to leave the arena and wait in his car for his son. One spectator who knew of this man's past incidents of offensive behaviour, told him he should attempt to get better control of himself if he was going to attend future hockey games. Muttering to himself the dejected parent cursed as he left the building.

Spectators don't always like the calls made by referees but should exercise caution in their remarks. Referees are the people who control the game to ensure that safety will prevail. This position entitles them to use quick decision-making to impose penalties for infractions which could lead to injuries. The new "Standards of Play" were introduced to limit physical injuries in a game. Hockey is a sport which requires complex skills. Those who partake in the game want to play the game without negative consequences, especially personal injury. When the referee makes calls because of aggressive behaviour, he ensures the safety of all players. Hockey parents must attempt to understand the importance of the referee's role and be willing to accept his calls in the best interest of the players.

CHAPTER FOUR

THE COACHES: THEIR IMPACT ON YOUNG HOCKEY PLAYERS

In the game of hockey, coaches come in different shapes and sizes. Some will assist your child in achieving their potential and others will cause more harm to your child's self-worth than you can imagine. At times you will have a choice in the selection of a coach. At other times you won't have the luxury of choosing a coach, and your child will be at the mercy of the person assigned to them. Hockey parents have to be cognizant of the different styles of coaching so they can decide which type is best for their child. Parents must remember that the skills the child learns are determined by the type of practice the coach designs. Selecting a coach with a management style which does not include proper practices nor proper leadership could have a negative impact on your child.

I remember the first time my oldest son "hit the ice" in search of his dream team. He had learned to skate the winter of his fifth birthday and the following hockey season, with a little prompting from his family, had decided to embark on his minor hockey journey. A hockey association in our community had recently implemented a Tyke Development Program for children. It was described as a good program to teach kids some of the fundamentals of hockey. After making telephone contact with the hockey association, I went to the local office and signed my kid into the program. Shortly thereafter we proceeded to the arena for team selection. The coaches distinguished themselves by the colourful insignias attached to their hockey jackets. As the youngsters skated over the ice demonstrating their abilities, the coaches discussed their general expectations with the parents. They provided insight regarding their philosophy of skill development. Having played hockey many years prior, I asked some pertinent questions regarding skill development. My questions were answered succinctly and information was offered regarding the program. The coaches informed the parents about the skills they would teach our kids. Accordingly, these skills would equip the child for later hockey development as they moved from the Tyke to the Novice level.

The hockey selection tryouts were scheduled twice a week over the next two weeks. The kids were expected to attend all sessions and the coaches would then select them into their respective teams. Parents were informed that initially, the coach would choose the kids with the best skills and the kids with limited skills would be selected later. Every kid would eventually be assigned to a team. By this selection process, each team would have an equal distribution of skilled and unskilled players.

It is imperative in the early stage of hockey development that parents recognize their child's strengths and weaknesses. Hockey parents shouldn't get themselves into a panic because their child isn't the first kid picked to join a team. This is merely a responsible action by a coach, to ensure they have a balanced team of players. The weaker players are picked later in the selection process and coaches anticipate these players will acquire more skills throughout the season. These players will learn some of their skills through coach instruction and some by observation of the other highly skilled players. At the time, I realized the importance of hockey skills. Children are malleable and trained with the proper techniques, can show quick advancement in this sport. Hockey is like any other sport and must be nurtured in the child so they get the best out of this activity. Werner Helsen and his colleagues advocate that to become an elite athlete, a child must practice their skills for a minimum of 10 years to excel in the sport. Using the Werner Helsen calculation led me to believe that by the time my kid reached his sixteenth birthday, he would be at the pinnacle of his skill development. This is consistent with the notion that by the time a player is 16, coaches have a good idea of a kid's chance of excelling to higher level leagues. Kids with hockey talent are usually drafted to provincial teams by age 16.

Some parents like to start their kids in hockey at age 3 because they are ready at this age. You will remember one of the unwritten rules of hockey from the earlier chapter. "Don't force a child to play hockey until they are ready". My second son had attempted to skate at age 3 but could not maintain his balance on ice. Two years later he was better coordinated and ready to learn skating techniques. Hockey parents must bear in mind that not all kids are ready to skate at the same age. If your child can't skate early, don't worry about it. At the age of 4 my kid couldn't skate so instead he played indoor soccer. He played the sport over the winter months and by the following year at age 5, he had the agility to commence a Canskate program. One year later, at the age of 6 he made the transition to hockey. It is important to remember that a child must know how to skate before they start hockey. I often see young hockey players in the Tyke Development Program who struggle on ice because they don't know how to skate. Some of these minor hockey players are completely out of their element. Parents must understand that a child requires basic skating skills prior to commencing hockey. Without these, they will not have any motivation to learn the game of hockey and will spend their time reclining on the ice.

All children can learn to skate. I remember teaching my first son this activity at age 5. It was a back-breaking experience and should only be attempted by the physically fit. A better way for your child to learn to skate would be to enrol them in a Canskate Program. Expert instructors are employed in these programs to teach the fundamental skills to the child. The child is taught agility through jumping activities and learns to use coordination to maintain their balance. Play activities are included so the child is not only learning skills but also having some fun while they are on the ice. Over a three month period, my kid learned the essentials of skating. He spent the following three months practising these skills during public skating sessions at the arena. The following year when he enrolled in hockey, he was more advanced in skating skills than most of his peers. To complement his skating skills, this child spent many hours using his older brother's NHL computer games. By playing these simulated games, he learned the fundamentals of hockey, including passing and shooting the puck. It is my belief that by using these computer games he had learned many of the guiding principles of hockey. To add to his knowledge of the game, he practised shooting on his hockey net set up in the driveway. These skills placed him in a state of preparedness for the Tyke Development Program. After a month in Tyke development, my younger kid was moved to Novice because he was further advanced in skating and hockey skills than many of his 6 year old peers. My advice to parents who are thinking of enrolling their child into hockey would be as follows:

1) Ensure that your child learns to skate by encouraging their involvement in a skating program offered at the community arena.
2) Take your child frequently to public skating so they can practise their skills.

3) Purchase some of the latest NHL computer games so they can play these and learn some of the rules of hockey (ie. passing, shooting and scoring).

4) Buy your child a net and set it up in the driveway so he/she can practice their shots.

Minor hockey associations throughout North America espouse hockey skill development for its players. These organizations offer hockey development programs in their attempt to impart skills to the child. These techniques ensure children will learn skating and hockey drills. In this way, the hockey associations attempt to improve the child's talent as they progress through the levels of hockey. When my older son first embarked upon his development as a budding hockey player, he was interested in learning these techniques. His hunger for these skills would motivate him to learn these first hand from the coach. My kid believed that once he learned the skills and practised them diligently, he would in time become a good hockey player. This formula for attainment of hockey development is a useful one. In combination with other factors (ie. interest and motivation) this will expedite the development of a kid's hockey talents.

Coaches take on their leadership roles because they believe they have some skills to offer minor hockey players. The coach, for the most part, is on the ice to encourage and motivate the child to excel in the sport of hockey. Hockey parents must remember the guiding principle, "all kids are not created equal on the ice". This infers that all kids do not have the same level of talent. The coaches, will attempt to bring out the best in your child. Some coaches will be demanding and rigid, whereas other coaches will be encouraging and flexible in their expectations. Most coaches have the best intentions for minor hockey players and will attempt to develop the player in accordance with a hockey program.

Research has indicated there are a number of components which are unique to player development. Coaches will use these components to develop your child's skills. This formula would indicate there are certain requirements to maximize the skills of the young hockey player. The Hockey Development Formula can be summed up as follows:

HOCKEY DEVELOPMENT = INNATE SKILLS + PERSONALITY + MOTIVATION + INCENTIVES.

Where:

1) Innate skills = genetic factors that create sensory-motor, visual-spatial, body-kinesthetic and cognitive ability
2) Personality = underlying character traits that effect behaviour
3) Motivation = drive, interest, "heart"
4) Incentives = intrinsic and extrinsic rewards

Coaches are the driving force behind hockey skills and the approach they use will bring out the best in the player. Specific techniques are used by every coach in an attempt to develop skills in a child. During a kid's initiation into hockey (ie. Tyke development), the coach evaluates the child's ability. Some kids have innate skills imprinted in their genetic code which will be enhanced through training. According to research, genetic ability can be traced to the approximately 30,000 genes in one's DNA. Kids who exhibit advanced hockey skills have been imprinted with the underlying sensory-motor talent stamped into their genetic codes. The genetic material forms the protein in the body which becomes the building block for physiological development. Those who are advantaged by the right combination of genes will inherit the body material which allows them to excel in this sport. For example, kids who are born with the right genetic material have a combination of unique skills. These include sensory-motor, visual-spatial, body-kinesthetic, and cognitive processing skills which better equip them to excel in their hockey talent. These unique features allow for advanced skills in the following areas:

1) Sensory-motor skills; hand/stick coordination (ie."good hockey hands")
2) Visual-spatial skills; the visual ability to evaluate the play (ie."see the ice")
3) Body-kinesthetic skills; advanced skating skills (ie."good balance/wheels")
4) Cognitive processing skills; having the ability to mentally process the play quickly as it unfolds on the ice (ie."hockey smarts").

Some players inherit innate skills which allow them to excel at hockey. Conversely, some players have very few of these skills and other players have none of these particular skills. The child who is born with genetic talent should have a better outcome in hockey. In his research, W. Hopkins noted that heredity accounted for 50% of the contribution to athletic performance. This would imply the underlying genetic markers equip the athlete by providing him/her with biological material needed to develop the skills to excel in sport. Genetic material is needed to form the physiological components which are at the basis of sensory-motor, visual-spatial, body-kinesthetic and cognitive processing skills.

Some athletes are born with the genetic markers which enhance their development of skills needed to excel in this sport. These are the players who have advanced talent and easily move into the NHL and are classified as "Phenoms".

Other factors including physical maturation of the young athlete as determined by the month they were born, is also of some importance to hockey development. Werner Helsen and colleagues have noted birth date to be of particular importance, since children born in the earlier months of the year (ie. the first quartile), will physically mature faster than those players born in the later months (ie. last quartile). K. Anders Ericsson and colleagues believe some athletes are at an advantage because their birth date falls in the first quartile and can spend more time practising their sport and this will allow them to excel. Whether genetics is enhanced by the practice effect has yet to be determined by further research. One would assume that athletes who are naturally talented and spend more time practising will excel in their sport. Joseph Baker supports the notion of genetics and its contribution to athletic performance but believes their is some variability in the contribution this plays. It is his belief that all variables which are thought to enhance athletic performance would have to be individually evaluated to estimate their contribution toward talent development.

One must bear in mind that even children with innate hockey skills do not blossom into highly skilled players unless they practice these skills. Furthermore, the athlete without genetic imprinting can still play hockey at an advanced level. These children will have to work harder at skills that don't come naturally. There have been some hockey players without much talent who have made it to the big league. These players made it in this sport because of a combination of skills including determination and motivation for the game.

The coach can only do so much for the player. The young hockey player must have the necessary skills so the coach can assist with their development. The right personality is also essential if the player is going to have the right attitude and confidence for the game of hockey. Without the right personality traits it is difficult for players to focus on their game. Coaches can only do so much for the player. Zest for the game has to come from within the athlete. The motivation to succeed in minor hockey is partially influenced by one's character traits. These traits will effect the way one engages in the game of hockey. Personality traits are unique to the budding hockey player and like the sensory-motor, visual-spatial, body-kinesthetic, and cognitive processing skills, to some degree are acquired through genetics. The child who displays confidence and poise has some of the building-blocks needed for positive development in the game. The coach can work with the kid who has these traits and assist the player to develop their talent.

Many people in a child's life influence their personality style. These include hockey parents, coaches and teachers who interact with the child. Personality is also influenced by genetic factors. Tough-minded hockey players acquire their personality status to a certain degree from their genes. A "tough minded kid" is more likely to persist in his/her attempt to win a game, even though his team might be losing. The "tender-minded kid", is more likely to give up in the same situation. This is of importance to the coach who must strive to recognize which kids on the team have the right personality traits to perform under adversity without giving up. The tender-minded kid may not respond well to stressful situations because of their emotional disposition. In a highly pressured game, the tender-minded kid has difficulty focusing—the duress of the game causes this youngster to make errors in play. The tender-minded kid doesn't have the right combination of underlying personality traits to maintain a emotionally balanced attitude toward the game.

Another important variable that can have an effect on a player's performance on ice is known as motivation (aka. heart, drive or interest) for the game. Researchers have coined the term motivation to encompass those factors which encourage performance in the game. Although the coach attempts to instill a drive in his players, much of the energy to excel has to come from within the player. Motivation is the expressed drive to engage in an activity. It is the basis of the individual hockey player's spirit which creates their underlying need to play the game with zest. Psychological theorists would agree that motivation is at the basis of the drive state which encourages the output needed by the player in every game.

From the time of early infancy, there is a need to engage in primary drives (ie. eating and drinking fluids) in order to survive. In his research on drive states, Robert Beck noted that primary drives are encouraged by internal and external reinforcers. This would imply that since one needs food and water to live, they work diligently to obtain money to acquire these basic needs. In minor hockey, the player doesn't achieve money for their hard work. However, they obtain recognition from the coach who praises their diligent effort. By working hard in the game and achieving goals, assists, and wins, the player will get praise and recognition from the coach for their output. As the season progresses, the hockey player achieves status with their personal statistics and team standing. The minor hockey player learns that winning creates positive drive states. Players achieve more satisfaction from positive experiences than negative ones and so they work harder to win a game.

Activities which are positive experiences are generally perceived by children as being more rewarding. A child who has had a positive experience is more willing to engage in this activity in the future. Minor hockey players value their sport because it is fun and of merit. It is difficult for a coach to motivate children who don't have any interest in the sport. The coach can't force children to take an interest in hockey. Furthermore, kids who don't have fun in hockey will never do well at this sport. They lack the interest in performing well at hockey because they don't perceive it as a positive experience. Children who are forced to play hockey will go through the motions but will never have the "heart" (motivation), for the game. Without the "heart" to play hockey a child will never perform at 100 % output. Coaches cannot teach a child to be interested in hockey. This is something that comes from within and can only be reinforced if it is exhibited by the player.

The last variable in the "Hockey Development Formula" is known as Incentive. This is consistent with rewards a child obtains from the sport. Minor hockey players are not paid for their involvement in this sport. In the child's mind, hockey is rewarding because it provides them with a fun-filled activity. This type of reward is referred to as an intrinsic reward. This provides the "positive feelings" kids obtain from engaging in this activity. They like the game because of its tempo, skills, and the friends they gain from the experience. Intrinsic rewards are reinforcers which create personal satisfaction and good feelings while one is playing the game. The coach often encourages these intrinsic drives. Through their interactions with the young hockey player, coaches increase children's self-worth and make them feel good about themselves.

Other motivators at work in the game of hockey are known as extrinsic rewards. Kids like extrinsic rewards they can show others or hang on their walls. Trophies and medals nicely fit into this category. These extrinsic rewards are tangible motivators which are important to young hockey players. They provide feedback to the child regarding their output in the game of hockey. Kids receive extrinsic rewards for their involvement in hockey games and learn to appreciate the importance of these rewards.

The coach is the driving force behind the hockey player's development. The coach's perception of your child's skills and the way he challenges these through instruction on the ice, will either "make or break your child". The attitude, personality and reinforcement techniques a coach uses with your child will determine whether the player pursues this sport. If your child gets the wrong type of coach, it could imminently result in his/her loss of interest in this sport and he/she will be compelled to leave hockey prematurely. The attitude and behaviour of the coach could invariably be constructive or destructive to your child. As a hockey parent, you will have to do your homework to ensure your child obtains the right type of coach to meet their needs.

There are a number of factors that will facilitate your child's success in minor hockey. The parent should evaluate the child's natural skills for the game. Some kids will have natural talent at this sport;—whereas others will have to work diligently to gain the skills. In combination, the natural skills and the right personality will increase a child's motivation for the game. When the going gets tough on ice, the "tough-minded" child will give the game their best effort.

The coach has to be cognizant of the talent, personality and motivation of his hockey players. With this knowledge, the coach can understand the child's strengths and weaknesses. Furthermore by having some knowledge of the child's emotional capacity, (ie. the child's moods and their ability to handle frustration) can assist the coach in dealing with issues when they arise. Hockey parents can assist the coach who may not be aware of the inner turmoil of the child. Hockey parents know their child better than anyone else and should be the first to offer assistance to their child when problems arise.

Some children are at an advantage when it comes to learning new skills. These children are better coordinated at an earlier age and seem to integrate their body-muscle movement (ie. body-kinesthetic) better than others. Some children naturally develop at a faster rate than others because of better coordination of their underlying physiological skills. For example, your child must know how to skate well in order to become a good hockey player. If your child is still struggling with backward skating, lateral manouvers or crossovers, they may lack that fine-motor coordination needed to execute skills and advance in hockey development. Every parent has to realize that a coach is not at the hockey arena to teach skating, but to assist the child in perfecting their hockey skills through practises. As a hockey parent, it is your responsibility to ensure that your child undertakes the programs that will teach them skating techniques. It is the coaches job to assist the child in learning the strategies that will advance their skill development in hockey.

Hockey parents often expect too much from the coach. Parents take their children to "tryouts" with the expectation the child will make a Double A or Triple A team. Parents become frustrated and angry when their children are not selected. In many cases, children attempt tryouts when they do not have the skating skills to play at the Double A or Triple A level. Often times, parents have never taken the child to any "skating programs" nor taken them to public skating where they could practise these skills. Hockey parents have to be apprised of the value of skating, if they want their child to excel in hockey. Parents must realize that children will never excel in hockey if they can't skate. Before a child can walk, he or she has to learn to crawl. Before a child can play hockey, he/she must learn to skate.

The emotional attitude that your child brings to the practise or game is also of importance to the coach. If your child does not feel good about themselves, has low self-esteem, or cannot take constructive criticism, hockey may not be their game. Coaches are informed by their Hockey Association to impart fair-play. In fact, all coaches are expected to undertake a CHA Speak Out Program which espouses this principle. This program instructs the coach to maintain a positive attitude toward children who play hockey. For the developing Tyke player, the proper verbal tactics and knowledge disseminated by the coach can lead to a positive experience. Coaches have to be aware of their impact on minor hockey players.

CHOOSING A COACH:

At the initiation level of hockey development children should be given fair ice-time. At the Tyke development level for example, clocks are sounded after short-shifts to ensure players get equal time on the ice. As minor hockey becomes more competitive, coaches involved in Double A and Triple A hockey don't always use a fair ice-time policy. Coaches at these levels of competitive hockey do not espouse fair time on the ice because their focus is on winning the game. Some children have a difficult time with this concept. A number of personal factors including level of self-esteem, sensitivity and motivation to play competitive hockey, will often colour the young player's interest in the game. Hockey parents have to face the fact that some children do not have the right temperament to engage in competitive hockey. They have difficulties with the game tactics used by coaches at this level. Some players do not want to engage in hockey when it is competitive and the coach is demanding and autocratic.

During hockey games, ranging from Novice to the Triple A divisions, I have observed coaches yelling at and criticizing young hockey players because of their on-ice activity. The way the child reacts to these situations appears to be consistent with their temperament. Some players respond by working harder, so they can get the coach off their backs. Other kids cannot cope with emotionally charged coaches who shout at them and become distraught by this experience. The personality and emotional constitution of the child can lead to a crippling experience. Some children are born emotionally fragile and do not have the tough minded attitude necessary to withstand the verbal onslaught of the coach. The parent should have some understanding of coaching style so they can recognize its possible impact on their child.

During a child's formative years, the parent spends countless hours in the nurturing process. This provides the parent with an understanding of the child's personality traits, emotional disposition and their ability to respond to situations. Hockey parents understand their child's ability to cope with excessive demands. During hockey games coaches yell and may use negative remarks as a way of motivating young hockey players. Some kids are not able to cope with this emotional abuse. Parents have to deal with the impact of the coach's criticism on the child. In the event the child has a tough-time with this management style, the hockey parent will have to counsel the child to ensure they are capable of coping with the coach's tirades.

There are different styles of leadership which are used in the management of people. Russell Cassel and Edward Stancik developed the Leadership Ability Questionnaire to evaluate these different styles. From my observation of hockey coaching staff, I have noticed these styles of leadership in operation and believe they can have an impact on a child's performance. Young hockey players depending on their emotional disposition, can adapt to some of these styles but not to others. For example, a coach who uses a rigid and demanding approach could have a negative impact on your child if he or she is tender-minded. In other words, some coaching styles may not be right for your child. The best thing a hockey parent can do, is to ensure their child has the best coach to suit their needs. This can be done by researching those people who coach hockey in your child's minor hockey league. The parent can make a list of prospective coaches available at your child's level and evaluate their style of coaching. Hockey parents in your community can assist you because of their past experience with these coaches. The type of leadership style the coach espouses and their philosophy regarding hockey will allow you to decide whether it is suitable for your child. There aren't any easy rules that you can follow in your decision regarding coach selection. You must always bear in mind that as the parent, you know your kid best. You have learned over the years about your child's emotional, mental and physical capabilities. Once you have evaluated all factors, then you can decide on the type of coach that will be the "best fit" for your child.

After meeting the coach, the parent becomes cognizant of the skills and techniques that will be used by the coach to instruct the child. The coach can highly influence your child over the countless hours they spend in practise and games. The decision you make regarding the selection of the coach, should be based on the needs of the child. Your child requires a coach who will train them in the hockey techniques which will make them adaptive at their level of hockey. The child needs to learn competency in their skills during their formative years of hockey development.

Minor hockey players have a dream they will make it to the big league. A coach with the right expertise can assist your child in achieving their dream. Your child must learn to effectively play the game of hockey and, at the same time, value the game as a recreational pursuit. Some coaches will assist children in learning skills, and at the same time, allow them to have some fun in the game. Other coaches will use excessive demands which might destroy your child's interest in the game. Your child should be assisted by the coach to develop their skills in hockey and should not be emotionally destroyed in the process. It is imperative that a hockey parent does not allow his or her child to undergo an "emotionally debilitating experience" while they learn the game of hockey. By doing some homework, a parent can obtain a coach that will function with the child's best interests in mind.

A parent must always remember that during practises and games their child is under the coach's influence and control. Your child however, will be returning home after the game, and you will be in charge of parenting long after hockey is done. The coach does not own your child during practises or games but is merely there to teach hockey skills. Time spent with a coach can either be a positive or a negative experience. The parent must be cautious in their selection of the person who coaches their child. Often there isn't much input into the selection process because hockey associations dictate who they select as coaches. I have met parents who have extracted their kid from a team and sought out an alternate person because of the negative impact of the coach on their child. I have also encountered parents who collectively hired and paid a person to coach their kids. These people couldn't find a coach with the characteristics they believed would assist in their children's hockey development.

Parents have to make decisions regarding their children's minor hockey career. They have to consider a kid's talent and the options available to them. They have to acknowledge their child's emotional and physical skills needed to play hockey. The parent has to ensure the child wants to venture beyond House League hockey and play at a competitive level. Some parents have high expectations for their child but often the child does not display natural talent in the hockey arena. Many parents realize their children do not have the skills nor the interest in pursuing high level competition. Others do not like demanding coaches, and complain they have been treated unfairly by the coach. These parents complain their children are sensitive and don't have the proper disposition to cope with the demands of a vociferous coach.

Children who cannot perform at a skill-level commensurate with that required by a team will not get much ice-time. This leads to frustration for the child and a decision to leave the team. If your child decides to quit hockey, this decision should be respected. It is the parent's responsibility however, to ensure the child's decision is based on relevant facts and not a result of an emotional response. Some children may want to continue with hockey but may need to relinquish their membership with a highly competitive team, which is not consistent with their personal talent.

The parent has to realize that coaches have different personality styles. An easy going coach is not a threat to the child or hockey parent. On the other hand a tough-minded, negative, vociferous and demanding coach can have a debilitating impact on your child. Destructive criticism at an early age, when the child is learning emotional boundaries, may be an excessive burden for the child to bear. A demanding coach could lead to "emotional instability" in the child. Children who are emotionally traumatized by coaches develop feelings of shame, doubt and inferiority. A negative hockey experience during the early developmental years could have a long-lasting and debilitating effect on your child's ego.

Choosing the coach that is best for your child isn't any easy feat. There are so many variables and only so much time the parent has to engage in this endeavour. Talking to other parents could provide you with some insight. However, you will still have to evaluate the style of coaching that is available in your hockey community. Weighing these alternatives and estimating which coach, team or hockey organization will meet your child's expectations should allow you to make the best decision. If your decision does not pan out then the best thing you can do is learn from your mistakes. Parents will have to ensure their future selection of a coach is not flawed by similar information processing errors. I have talked to parents whose choice of coach did not work out for their child. This led to the child's decision to quit the team before the season was over. In the end, this was disastrous because the child had been enthusiastic about playing hockey.

Once you and your child have settled on the selection of a coach and team, attempt to stay with the team until the end of the hockey season. I have encountered parents who have taken their child out of hockey prior to the completion of the year. This quick decision was made by the hockey parent because of conflict with the coach. The parent and/or the child were not getting along with the coach because of excessive demands and limited ice-time. Rather than attempting to resolve the situation, a hasty response was made to remove the child. Removing your child from a team, prior to the completion of the hockey season sends a negative message to the child. This message implies "if things don't work out, you can quit". This is not a positive learning experience for the child. Children have to learn early in life that personal experiences are not always positive. Life is not always a bowl of cherries;—you can't always pick your boss, co-workers or neighbours, but you can do your best to get along with people. If your choice of coach doesn't work out, the parent can do the best to minimize conflict for their child.

Hockey parents should provide positive messages to their

children. These could include the notion of adaptability, resilience and persistence, especially when the going gets tough. A list of things that you can teach your child during their hockey experience are as follows:

1) If things are not going well, work harder to improve them.
2) If the coach continues to pick on you, show him that you are much better at hockey than he thinks.
3) If you are not selected as a first line player, don't worry about it, but work harder to prove that you are a solid team player.

A child has to learn that life's experiences can be positive or negative. Emotional maturity can be gained from experiences in which one has to adapt and handle pressure. Children can learn from every situation and this will allow them to grow emotionally. Small steps are required as one attempts to obtain their goals in life. To get along with others, the child has to adjust to the demands of the situation. Life is about these adaptive experiences. The child has to learn the expectations of others and work diligently in order to achieve these goals.

Minor hockey is not always a positive experience, but a lot of hard work. Hockey parents must impart this message to the child. Many of the experiences or frustrations in hockey are no different than other situations in life. No one can predict where they will be in twenty years time. The 8 year old child is continually learning new experiences and should look to every day as a challenge. People learn from the challenges and the demands that others place on them. The parent has to teach the child to be a "striver and not a quitter". Hockey parents have to impart concrete messages to the child and foster development so they can prepare the youngster for life's voyage.

KNOWING THE COACHES EXPECTANCIES:

Every parent and every minor hockey player should know the coach's expectancies. These should be laid out at the beginning of the hockey season by the coach. If these expectancies aren't discussed, the parent should make an inquiry about these. For example, if the coach decides on equal ice-time for every hockey player, this plan must be followed throughout the season. Conversely, if the coach places greater emphasis on "winning the game" and decides that ice-time is dependent on "output and motivation" of the child while on ice, then this should also be clearly adhered to throughout the hockey season. There is no greater frustration for parent or kid, than a hockey coach who does not clearly spell out their philosophy of play and then introduces new rules as the season progresses. Changing the expectancies only creates frustration for the child and aggression by the parent.

I have observed situations in which the coach did not provide clear expectancies to the hockey parent and player. One particular example comes to mind. In this scenario the coach had defined his expectancies at the beginning of the hockey season and stated that all kids would receive fair ice-time. The only exception that would prevail was during power plays and penalty killing. At these times only talented players would see the ice. The coach noted that he would only place kids on the ice who were capable of performing at a high-level of output. Furthermore, he would choose only those hockey players whom he believed to have better talent and skills.

The hockey season had been going well under this coach's leadership but at one game, he decided to change his rules of play. The coach decided to expand his rules, and benched many hockey players because he wanted to beat the competing team. Some kids seldom saw the ice and spent much of their time "riding the pine". One must remember that the coach had selected players at the beginning of the season because of their talent. He later changed his principles of fair ice-time because he wanted to improve the team's standing. Since many players were not getting equal time on the ice they complained openly to the coach. Some parents also expressed outrage because of the changes in the coach's plan. By changing the agreed upon plan, the coach had not only frustrated the young hockey players but had also frustrated the parents. The prevailing verbal aggression by hockey kids and their parents was understandable and consistent with the theory of Frustration-Aggression advocated by John Dollard and his colleagues. This theory stipulates that frustration caused by unexpected changes in routines, creates an instability in emotion. When this occurs, it will lead to aggression against the person or thing that has caused the frustration.

You must remember that hockey players are selected for their skills. These skills are exhibited during the tryouts at the beginning of the season. The level of skill and performance demonstrated by the player leads to their selection by a team. All developing hockey players require fair ice-time. As previously noted, the only exception which should prevail occurs during power plays and/or penalty killing. Hockey parents should confront coaches when changes are made to existing plans without an explanation. This is especially of importance when the child first commences hockey (ie. Tyke, Novice and Atom) because young hockey players require time on ice to perfect their skills. Confrontation of the coach can be done civilly and without heated discussion. The point that I want to raise here is that hockey kids, parents and coaches must remember that expectancies have to be clearly laid out at the beginning of the season and these have to be closely followed. Once hockey players and their parents are apprised of the rules, these have to be adhered to by all members of the team, including the coach.

When "rules of play" are clear to hockey players and their parents, then it is much easier to evaluate the objectives of the team. This should be done before signing a card with a team. The coach should not change the rules as the season progresses. If there are changes to be made, these should be done only after the issues have been addressed. Changes in the rules should only be implemented after they have been discussed with all members present. A coach should not cancel a player from fair ice-time unless this message was clear at the start of the season. There are many ramifications and negative outcomes for hockey players, parents and coaches, when objectives are not discussed and changes implemented.

Conversely, every parent should bear in mind that once they have agreed and committed to the objectives laid out by the coach, then they should follow this plan. I have observed situations where the coach made it quite clear at the beginning of the hockey season that a "player's ice-time" would be decided by the type of motivation they displayed while they were on ice. Robert Beck has described motivation as a drive that is determined by choice, persistence and vigour of goal directed behaviour. Exhibiting energetic output during the game, demonstrates to others that a hockey player has the motivation to play the game. The message is clear and signifies to the coach that the hockey player is interested and has the expected drive state to give 100% during the game.

Much to the chagrin of hockey players and parents, is the resulting frustration when some players don't get much time on the ice. Coaches constantly evaluate their players output, and when performance is not up to par, players are relegated to the bench. Hockey parents have to be realistic. They must accept the mandate of the coach when the players are not working diligently. Those who don't perform with the utmost motivation do not deserve to be on the ice. When the coach clearly lays out rules of play, these have to be adhered to so that players understand the consequences of poor performance on the ice. For some coaches, the main objective of the game is to win at all costs. Life isn't fair and neither is ice-time given by coaches who have as their mandate, "winning the game". Hockey is a team sport and only with the use of every player can the game be won. At the same time however, hockey parents have to realize that a certain level of performance is expected of all players. If this effort isn't forthcoming, then the coach should make decisions that will ensure the best success for the team. If that means benching the player, parents have to concede to this decision. Clear objectives are necessary and plans should be executed to reflect these outcomes. Hockey players and parents need clear objectives and expectations. These factors allow them to cope with decisions. When objectives or expectancies are changed, it only creates stress and conflict. Objectives in a hockey game are based upon short-term and long-term goals. These goals can only be achieved when hockey parents and minor hockey players have knowledge of the expectancies.

To appreciate the effectiveness of coach and hockey player interaction, it is important for the hockey parent to understand the mechanism of coaching style. With this information, sound decisions can be made by the parent in advance of signing a child to a team. Decision-making about hockey team selection should not be left to the child. As noted earlier, children by virtue of their level of cognitive development, do not have the abstract reasoning ability to make sound decisions. Research by neuroscientists would concur that the human brain is not fully formed until the young adult is approximately 20 to 25 years of age. Specifically, the frontal area of the brain that is involved in decision-making does not reach its fullest potential of reasoning until early adulthood. This occurs because the neural matter in the frontal brain has not fully matured. This would imply that children do not have the planning strategy nor reasoning to make complex decisions. It is therefore up to the parent to evaluate the coaches expectancies. After assessing the mandate of the coach and the team philosophy regarding rules of play, then a decision could be made to sign or not sign your child to the team. If the rules are not clear, obtain the data in writing, so that you and your child understand the contractual agreement before completing the team registration card.

EVALUATING THE COACHES' STYLE OF LEADERSHIP:

In this section, I will discuss the concept of leadership. Insight into this area, will allow the parent to understand the coach's style of leadership. Parents need to understand the strategies which are imparted by the coach. These provide one with a level of comfort because they allow parents to know what to expect from the coach. Having some knowledge of the coach's style is beneficial because the parent would then be assured of the style of leadership used to assist the child in learning hockey skills.

Parents are aware of different styles of leadership. They are exposed to these in their workplace, and often times have experienced the impact of these styles. Some styles of leadership are beneficial whereas others are harmful. Most parents in the work force do not have the luxury of picking their boss. When the boss is not the right fit, this can lead to a disastrous impact on the employees. Adults experience conflict in the work force because some bosses use tactics which are not always conducive to the objectives of the organization. For example, those who use "bullying tactics" cause stress to the employee and this can lead to debilitating consequences.

The same parallel can be made with situations in which

kids are subjected to coaches with aversive leadership styles. Not all coaches are the best fit for the child. Hence, these situations must be evaluated to ensure that a child is not exposed to a troublesome coach who will have an adverse effect on the child. Children are not designed with the "same mould" and cannot tolerate similar demands. Coaches can create pressure for youngsters and this can lead to negative consequences. What is good for one child, is not universally good for all children. Hockey parents can appreciate the fact that certain styles of coaching may not be well tolerated by every child. This infers that parents have to be selective in choosing a coach. This can be done by evaluating the hockey coaches available in the league, and learning about the style of leadership they will impose on the team.

Joseph Baker and his colleagues have noted that coaches are generally involved in the training process and therefore have a significant impact on the athlete. These researchers posit that in team sports for example the certain styles of coaching are more beneficial than others. Others including P. Terry and B. Howe would indicate that in team sports, the autocratic style is the preferred method of dealing with athletes. Other researchers including Susan Butt would indicate that in situations where there is a poor relationship between the coach and the athlete, the performance level of the athlete will decrease. Still others including N. Barnett and his colleagues showed that when the coach and the athlete had a good relationship and good interaction there was less of a likelihood of the athlete quitting the sport.

There are many different styles of coaching, but the most common ones that I have observed in the arena appear to fit into four general styles of leadership. Some coaches may be eclectic and use combinations of these styles to provide leadership to young hockey players:

1) Autocratic
2) Authoritative
3) Democratic
4) Laissez-faire.

These styles of leadership are based on the work of Russell Cassel and Edward Stancik. I have adapted these leadership styles after careful reflection on the behaviour exhibited by coaches in minor hockey. It is my impression the hockey parent will find these useful in evaluating coaching styles available in their community.

AUTOCRATIC COACH:
When I think about the autocratic coaching style, my perception is that of a coach who is demanding and has high expectancies. These coaches impart excessive rules and high expectations in their effort to maximize winning. They will not spare a child's feelings in their effort to beat the opponent team. Coaches who use this style are found in House League, Double A and Triple A divisions. This type of coaching style is tantamount to what is known as the "boot-camp-drill-sergeant". Hockey parents come to realize this coaching style as being consistent with an approach known as a "demanding style of leadership". Some children can function under this pressured style because they appreciate rigid direction and orders.

Even though the autocratic style has its merits, it is best used with hockey players who are older and have better developed egos and high levels of self-esteem. These older players have the ability to cope with the pressure of a demanding coach. By the time a child has reached mid-adolescence, he or she should have a reasonable level of self-worth and should not be emotionally bruised by the negativity of the coach. I have observed kids who have "emotionally folded" under the pressure of the autocratic coach. Kids who are exposed to this model would possibly quit hockey before their adolescence because they could not withstand the emotional abuse of the coach.

Children who respond positively to the autocratic coaching style do so because they like direction. They enjoy a style of leadership that is rigid and task-oriented. Some children who are tough-minded have the right personality to adjust to the autocratic coaching style. These children appreciate challenges and don't waiver when the coach barks out orders. Some hockey players respond well to an autocratic leader because they like an approach which is directive and rule-oriented. These young hockey players are willing to put their trust in the coach and carry out plans. A child who is emotionally solid (ie. tough-minded) would fit in well with this model of coaching. This child would likely have a desire to follow the demands of the coach because he or she adheres to the notion that the coach knows best. This coaching style would be accepted by many who appreciate military models. The tough-minded child can cope with the tirades and emotional pressure exerted by the coach. These type of hockey kids perceive demands as a challenge and this would motivate them to measure up to the coach's expectations, by working diligently in competitive play.

The autocratic style would not be readily accepted by emotionally sensitive children. Children who have difficulty functioning in a highly demanding environment, replete with duress and emotional stress, would not thrive. The leadership imparted by a coach who espoused tough verbal tactics would cause these sensitive-minded kids to falter. Some children do not thrive on the boot-camp-model. They do not enjoy a coach who barks out orders. These children do not benefit from a rigid style which does not provide options nor choices.

Raymond Cattell and his colleagues have developed two questionnaires (ie. Cattell Personality Questionnaire and the Sixteen Personality Factor Inventory) to analyze personality styles. These psychometric tests have been used to evaluate underlying personality traits of children and adults and can be administered by psychologists who are registered with provincial or state associations. They can be administered prior to enrolling kids on a team. By having the child undertake these tests, the psychologist can provide the parent and the coach with an overview of the child's personality characteristics. This would provide an understanding of the individual's personality dynamics. With this information, the parent and the coach would have some knowledge of the emotional pressure a child might withstand as hockey players. Kids are not created with the same personality traits. Some kids are adaptive and some are not; some kids can deal with orders and others can not. The parent should have knowledge of their child's personality or bear the consequences of placing the child on a team where conflict and pressure may bruise the child's ego.

Autocratic coaches tend to be demanding of hockey players in their zealousness to reach the ultimate goal of winning. These coaches will favour the team's importance over the needs of the individual child. Consequently, children who are not able to withstand the emotional abuse of the coach may not have the ability to measure up to this autocratic style. Some children would emotionally suffer at the hands of the autocratic coach because they cannot handle verbal abuse. The ultimate insult to the sensitive child would arise when they are yelled at, referred to as "stupid", or punished by "riding the pine" because they performed poorly on the ice. The autocratic coach may reward the player by verbally praising them for hard work and excellence but this praise might not occur often enough for the emotionally sensitive child. Sensitive children would not do well under this style of guidance. These kids would exhibit emotional upset and demonstrate tension, anxiety, worry and fear of the coach.

Hockey parents have to be open-minded to the needs of their children and remember that the autocratic coach is not the best fit for the child if he or she is emotionally sensitive. Hockey parents experience a sense of discomfort when they see their child being "put down" by the coach. The sensitive child also experiences a level of discomfort and this creates personal anxiety. An autocratic coach who uses this harsh style of management as a way of motivating or encouraging the team to excel, may not be acting in the best interest of the child. At its worst, this type of coaching could destroy your child's enthusiasm to play hockey because it causes stress, anxiety, fear and lowered self-esteem.

AUTHORITATIVE COACH:
The authoritative coach is the type of person many hockey kids would like to have coaching them. Like authoritative parents, this coach influences behaviour by a management style which is based on knowledge and direction. A coach who uses the "authoritative philosophy" is apt to provide the child with structure and the means of obtaining goals. This type of coach would be reluctant to use a "dictatorial style" of management that appears consistent with that used by the autocratic coach. The authoritative coaching style is reflective of leadership which allows for enrichment of the child. This coaching technique permits the child to learn from a coach who is well versed on the implementation of hockey skills. Authoritative coaches use their expertise in hockey to shape up skills of the individual and the team. They provide feedback to their players but do not use a "dictatorial method" to impart these skills. The authoritative coach utilizes a repetitive manner rather

than screaming out the demands to the hockey player. The authoritative coach is supportive and uses praise to shape up personal and team skills. Practices are laid out with the expectancy the hockey player will learn these skills. When the hockey player fails to understand the tactics, the authoritative coach does not scream at the player but reminds them of the strategies that must be used to complete the drill effectively.

Many kids do well with an authoritative style of coaching. Observation of the autocratic and authoritative coaching styles would indicate many differences in these coaching styles. My oldest kid has played hockey for 10 years and during this time I observed many styles of coaching. When I reflect back to the kids who were initially involved in Tyke development, I am aware of only 5 youngsters from my son's original Tyke team who are still playing hockey at an organized level. Statistically speaking, this represents about 38% of the original team. Apparently this is a high percentage, given the attrition rates found in minor hockey. The kids who quit hockey probably lost interest in this sport or pursued other endeavours. The impact of coaching style on a child's decision to quit hockey could be evaluated through longitudinal research.

Northern Ontario has a lengthy winter season. There are many indoor arenas and outdoor rinks in the northern communities. Many children skate or play hockey as a form of recreation. Many kids who become involved in hockey commence this activity by playing Tyke development and continue until the Midget level. Many will quit hockey over this ten year period and seek out other activities. With maturity other interests take over and because of these pursuits a different set of goals may emerge for adolescents. For those kids who like to play hockey, it is my impression that hockey parents need to be selective in their choice of coaches. Parents may want to seek out a coach who uses an authoritative style of coaching.

Enrolling your child on a team with an authoritative coach will enable the child to experience a style of leadership which provides positive direction and skills. During their early years of hockey, this will facilitate personal and emotional growth.

DEMOCRATIC COACH:

Democratic coaches are unique in their own way. As this style of leadership implies, the "democratic coach" allows for equal opportunity for all hockey players. This form of coaching is an ideal approach for minor hockey players and has its merits. The democratic coach, is willing to use a management style which imparts fairness to all players on a team. In Tyke development this couldn't be a better way of operating a minor hockey team. Every child comes to the rink with a desire to learn the rudimentary skills of hockey. Giving each child the opportunity to engage in these skills provides an equitable learning experience.

Every kid who plays hockey deserves equal opportunity and respect. This appears to be a mandate of the democratic style of coaching. This style of leadership is important in minor hockey because it does not create favouritism. At about age 9, many children commence Atom level hockey. Greater demands are placed on children at this age as they adapt to the rigours of competitive level hockey and learn the skills that will allow them to advance to Double A hockey teams. As the child becomes more adaptive and skilled at the game of hockey, there is an inherent rule which implies that children with better hockey skills should be given the opportunity to excel. Better hockey players are consequently allowed more ice-time and this attitude generally prevails in most hockey associations.

Coaches have to be willing to bring out the best in children who play hockey so they can excel in their skills. Much to the chagrin and envy of some hockey parents, not all kids are created with the same hockey talent. Differences observed in kids appear to be a function of what some researchers refer to as advanced hockey talent. Translated into layperson's terms, this means some children have better "hockey hands, hockey smarts and see the ice better" than others. Children who possess these skills have more specialized talent which allows them to adapt to the ice. The basis of this talent is found in the child's genes. A child with natural hockey talent is given more latitude by coaches in demonstrating skills. This comes in the form of allowing more time on ice in regular games, in tournaments and during play-offs.

Autocratic coaching styles use rigid demands whereas authoritative coaches use knowledge based principles to manage their hockey team. The democratic coach is different because he or she uses a style that provides equal opportunity to all children. They utilize knowledge-based techniques and provide a leadership style which is open and receptive to the needs of the players. Democratic coaches want every kid to have equal opportunity and fair ice-time. This is beneficial to self-esteem building in the child. The only problem with this approach, is that fair-play tactics may not allow the democratic coach to win many games. The style of thinking, which separates the democratic coach from the former two coaching styles, is beneficial where fun is the expected outcome.

In hockey leagues where team standing and winning prevail, there is a greater need to push for "wins" at all costs. Even at the preliminary level of hockey, house league coaches like to win games and tournaments. In the event the parent wants his or her kid to have equal opportunity and fair ice-time, they have to realize the democratic coaching style does have its costs. A hockey parent who is only interested in "equal opportunity" should register their child in a league that values "fun" and is not concerned with the outcome of winning. To ensure that a child has a greater opportunity for development of skills, the hockey parent must be willing to put their child in a higher level of competitive hockey. This means allowing the child with hockey talent to move to the rank of Double A or Triple A teams. With this expectancy, the parent then has to realize that at the higher level of competition comes a different coaching style. This might include the principles of autocratic or authoritative coaching styles.

Hockey parents must bear in mind that the democratic coach is a good choice of coaching style for the young developing child. The techniques espoused by this coach include praise and fair ice-time to encourage development of the young hockey player. Democratic coaches encourage their players to learn skills and develop cooperative team work. These types of coaches attempt to balance the needs of the individual players with the needs of the team. They will at times allow their highly skilled players more time on the ice but this is generally relegated to the last minutes of play, power plays, or overtime situations.

The focus of the democratic coach might be to win but not at all costs. The feelings of the individual player are taken into consideration and every child will have equal time on the ice. Positive reinforcers generally in the form of praise or "high fives" are given throughout the game to reward the child's effort. If criticism is delivered it is given in a constructive manner. It tends to be included during "team talk" so that a player isn't centred out. All members of a minor hockey team benefit from this model of coaching. Many hockey parents like this style of coaching for their kids because it tends to be positive and constructive. Coaches who advocate this style are especially beneficial to young hockey players who are developing an appreciation for the game of hockey. For the tender-minded player this style of coaching offers a style which builds personal and emotional needs through positive experiences.

Democratic coaches are generally receptive toward teaching new ways of challenging their players in higher level play. They use positive skills that will encourage young hockey players. They are open-minded and seem to have a willingness to teach new strategies that will improve their players' skills. They perceive the hockey arena as a setting which builds experiences through cooperation and fairness to all kids. These coaches are ready to take on challenges and enthusiastically endorse equal rights of all players. The moto of the democratic style would likely espouse "equal opportunity through fair ice-time".

LAISSEZ FAIRE COACH:
The last type of coaching style is probably the least effective of all styles of coaching in competitive hockey. This particular type of coach is likely to serve as a figure head on the bench. These coaches will work toward the development of the child but at the same time impart the message that "everybody should have fun". Non-competitive kids who are involved in recreational hockey would benefit most from this coaching style. This type of coach is not interested in rigid strategies but essentially is on the bench to make sure everyone is getting fair ice-time and having fun. There would be little need to provide much feedback to kids other than to ensure there weren't too many kids on the ice at one time.

The Laissez-faire type of approach is tantamount to that style of coaching found in weekend pick-up games. In these situations, youngsters gather at the local outdoor rink and throw their sticks into a pile for selection onto a team. Players take their turns on the ice and not much strategizing takes place other than kids cooperatively working together to beat their opponents. The laissez-faire coach would be willing to allow his hockey players to take charge of activities on the ice with little need to develop team principles. Typically what would emerge are players who do their own thing and attempt to learn hockey skills through trial and error. This type of coach would not be suited for the highly competitive level of hockey but would best function in a non-competitive league or weekend pick-up game of hockey. Every member on this team would be allowed to have fun and develop their skills at their own discretion. In a nutshell, this is a great "pond hockey approach" but not of much benefit to competitive hockey where skills, team work and winning are the general focus of the game.

In summary, the aforementioned coaching styles seem to be the primary ones used to direct and instruct minor hockey players. Each style is unique and has its own merits. The autocratic and authoritative styles are the types of leadership models used in Double A and Triple A competitive hockey. Some coaches in House League hockey also use these styles of coaching because they are intent on winning. Democratic and laissez-faire leadership styles are also of use, but are generally limited to the developmental stages of hockey where fun and skill development are needed. It is important for parents and coaches to realize that the last two models are necessary and should be primarily used for minor hockey players who are at the early stages of hockey development and don't need emotional pressure.

CHAPTER FIVE

MOTIVATING YOUR CHILD TO PLAY HOCKEY

To play the game of hockey well, one must have some interest and love for the game. Hockey players must have heart and determination to do their best when they are on the ice. Even in the minor league, kids have to be motivated to enhance their performance on ice. From the time young athletes commence involvement in this sport, there is a need to understand the motivational variables that encourage one to play hockey. Having discussed this issue with the young players, a multitude of reasons emerge for their involvement in hockey:

1) fun
2) better than going to school
3) hockey allows them to play with friends
4) learn skills
5) compete with other teams
6) gain respect from peers
7) impress others (ie. coaches, parents, friends)
8) physical activity
9) tournaments
10) want to make it to the NHL

A discussion with hockey parents indicates they also have reasons for encouraging their child's pursuit of this sport. Many parents want their children playing hockey because it provides them with physical activity. Furthermore, parents believe the game of hockey will allow their children to develop friendships and learn ways of cooperating with others. Some parents believe that involvement in hockey is a good way of ensuring their child avoids relationships with an undesirable peer group. Last, some parents believe that hockey will take their child to stardom in the NHL.

Hockey kids and their parents are interested in hockey because this sport provides positive attributes that will assist the child in their personal development and make them skilled hockey players. To make this happen, parents are willing to invest large sums of money so their kids can become accomplished athletes. This altruistic attitude of parents who sacrifice their time, energy and money, is the reason that many young hockey players become involved in this sport. Hockey parents can only be commended for their caring attitude and their willingness to provide their kids with the opportunity to develop themselves. This ultimate spirit of support by the parent is at the basis of a child's success in hockey.

Research has shown that coaches provide a major impetus by teaching players skills that are necessary in this sport. To undertake this role, it is imperative the coach has insight regarding the young hockey player's commitment. According to the research of J. Holbrook and J. Barr, the coach must be prepared to evaluate personality and psychological status of athletes prior to placement in specific hockey leagues. Every kid does not arrive on the hockey scene with the same interests, drives or aspirations. The factors that motivate the child in the game of hockey must be clear to the coach. Most children become involved in this sport at the Tyke Development level. As the child's skills increase, he or she begins to evaluate the level of competition that is consistent with their skills. Some young players are only interested in House League hockey whereas others strive to attain Triple A level status. Some kids are only interested in weekend practises and games while others will expend maximum energy to obtain their ultimate dream of competitive hockey found in the NHL. The ability to self-motivate and spend the pre-season in preparation for a sport is considered to be a useful tactic for the athlete, especially for those at the competitive level. Saul Miller believes that prior to the hockey season, players should evaluate their objectives. This will assist them in preparing for the hockey season. For example, players who undertake pre-season initiatives including physical training, self-talk and imagery building will enhance their ability to perform well during the season. With specific goals, the athlete can work toward a game plan. Craig Stewart and Michael Meyers believe that athletes with higher skill levels who are internally driven to succeed at a sport, will do better in competition than those athletes with average skills and no internal motivation. Other researchers contend that some kids don't have the ability to motivate themselves and require ongoing direction to encourage their active involvement in hockey. These children learn best when coaches and hockey parents reinforce their on-ice activity. Hockey parents with knowledge of reinforcement theory can provide the necessary encouragement and praise to their child. According to David Bergin and Steven Habusta, minor hockey players between the ages of 10 and 13 tend to be more ego-oriented in their approach to hockey. They need input from important others (ie. coaches, parents) so they can apply their knowledge to a game plan. Their limited reasoning skills prevent them from objectively evaluating the team's goals. Kids at this age tend to be ego-focused, and believe that a coach will use mistakes as a way of judging their on-ice performance. This could be disastrous, especially when children believe that poor play-making while they are on the ice will lead to less positive attention from the coach. These misbeliefs will inhibit the child's performance, because in their mind, every action on ice must be to perfection. Pre-adolescent youngsters believe it is better to make the perfect play rather than fail in their performance at this task. Their fear of failure tends to be a significant motivational factor. This can adversely impact on their game performance, because rather than attempting a shot at the net and fail, they believe it advantageous to not risk the shot. This fear of failure inhibits their performance and becomes the motivational factor which influences their shot-taking activity on ice.

Prior to adolescence, children are at the concrete stage of development. Their cognitive skills prevent them from fully appreciating the objectives set forth by the coach. Constantly repeating and informing the players of the team's directives is necessary to enhance player performance. The coach who continually reminds the young hockey player of their task and reinforces the child once this is accomplished, will provide the best impetus for player development. Young hockey players seek out encouragement from their parents and their coaches. The proper feedback to the player is imperative, as it not only assists with personal development but also serves as a mechanism for accomplishing the team objectives.

Research by David Bergin and Steven Habusta indicates that young hockey players experience conflict during their games. They often struggle with their needs to score goals and attempt to evaluate each play as it happens. They are often in conflict as they attempt to understand whether they should shoot or not shoot the puck. Unable to quickly resolve their dilemma, athletes hesitate to make a play because of this internalized conflict. According to Neal Miller, the approach-avoidance conflict interferes with behavioural output. In minor hockey, this conflict can become instrumental to a player's performance on-ice. For example, a player caught in the approach-avoidance conflict (ie. shooting the puck versus not shooting the puck) may hesitate in making a decision to react quickly to a on-ice situation. This hesitation in decision-making will sometimes interfere with the performance outcome of scoring a goal. By taking too much time to make a decision, because of conflict between one's approach-drive (eg. wanting to score a goal) and avoidance-drive (eg. believing a goal is impossible or having a fear of failure at scoring), lowers the hockey player's decision to take the shot. A player who functions as a forward is sometimes in conflict about shooting the puck. He may want to shoot the puck, but hesitates because he does not have the perfect shot at the net. His fear of failure will prompt him to hesitate. The split-second of hesitation can make the difference in scoring or not scoring a goal. A similar conflictual situation is experienced by defencemen who must respond effectively in a two on one rush. The defenceman may not be certain which man to block, the shooter with the puck or the man on the opposite wing. This hesitation costs the defenceman valuable time in decision-making. This could serve as a disadvantage, thereby costing the defenceman a positive outcome by not blocking the shot.

Research in the area of the motivational theory, especially conflict resolution (ie. approach-avoidance), infers that young athletes need to learn to focus on their objectives. Given the proper feedback from the coach, this should allow the hockey player information which will assist them with quick decision-making in the game. Minor hockey players should be less concerned with the perfect play and more concerned with their attempt at performing the skill to the best of their ability. The young athlete who is nurtured with reflexive thought processes through proper feedback from the coach will be satisfied with most of their play-making activities. In situations where they have to make quick decisions, they will work toward creative plays in their attempt to perform well. In this way they satisfy themselves and they satisfy the coach.

Coaches strive to increase the performance level of the team so there can be optimal output. There are many players on a team with different skill levels and personality styles. Coaches attempt to operationalize the best ways of motivating their team. William Revelle has aptly stated that "motivation is the link between knowing and doing; between thinking and action; between competence and performance". It is Revelle's belief that motivation is ultimately concerned with direction, intensity and duration of behaviour. In learning theory, this would imply that given a situation (performance) where the player has a shot at the net (stimulus), he/she uses cognitive skills (ie. thought processing) to bring about a solution (response). This in turn provides feedback to the player regarding their competence in performance of the task.

PERFORMANCE = STIMULUS + THOUGHT PROCESSING + RESPONSE

Some believe that motivating an athlete is a complex process. Stuart McKelvie and his colleagues have shown that athletic performance is determined by a number of factors (ie. physical training and personality) which are unique to the individual athlete. One must evaluate these variables in order to achieve the best outcome for the athlete. Research by Valliant and his colleagues, has demonstrated that personality is a highly influential factor which involves performance in athletes who participate in individual or team sports. The personality of the athlete has been found to have an impact on motivational level. Especially since personality traits enable the athlete to master "self-talk and utilize mental imagery", two of the guiding techniques used in self-motivation.

It is my hypothesis that performance can be maximized in young athletes if they are provided with the right mix of motivational factors. Clark Hull devised a model which has been of assistance in explaining performance in lower organisms. For example, Hull stated that motivation is an excitatory response that can be influenced by a number of factors. He used a mathematical model to explain his theory:

EXCITATORY RESPONSE (BEHAVIOUR/PERFORMANCE) = HABIT (LEARNED BEHAVIOUR) X DRIVE (MOTIVATION) X INCENTIVE (REWARD).

Hull's model was unique in describing the response output of lower organisms however, it could not account adequately for human performance. Humans have unique individual traits that drive their "inner spirit" during competition. Research by Stuart McKelvie and his colleagues support the notion that performance can be maximized in athletes when individual variables, including training methods and personality traits, are used to increase performance output. Based on models described by Hull and McKelvie, it is my impression that athletes are driven by a number of factors in their attempt to maximize performance. I would propose that a young hockey player's performance could be evaluated using the following model. I have described this in detail in the previous chapter.

HOCKEY PERFORMANCE = INNATE SKILLS +
PERSONALITY + MOTIVATION + INCENTIVE.

A hockey parent could use these combined factors to evaluate their child's performance. The hockey player's performance outcome can only be evaluated accurately once all of these factors have been determined. The individual components which comprise this model are as follows:

(1) Innate Skills = genetics, which enhance sensory motor, visual-spatial, kinesthetic and cognition.
(2) Personality = individual traits which influence output in a game.
(3) Motivation = "heart", personal drive, interest, past habits and learning experience.
(4) Incentives = internal and external rewards which influence the athlete's performance.

INNATE SKILLS:

Some kids are better hockey players than others. They have what coaches refer to as "hockey smarts". These kids have the innate genetic skills which equip them with the physiological traits that make them better hockey players. A child's genetic code holds the key to these inherited traits. Every person has approximately 30,000 genes; these genes are at the basis of the 23 pairs of chromosomes that every person possesses. The genes constitute the biological building blocks found in the cells of the body. These genes make the player adept at expressing their skills. Minor hockey players with advanced skills have been imprinted with the genetics that enhance their physiological make-up. This is in line with the research of C. Bouchard and his colleagues who found that genetics account for 50% of an athlete's ability. Consistent with the heredity argument, W. Hopkins has found that physical factors especially height may be explained by 80% of the genetic variance. Genes contribute to physical development, and talented athletes are born with these specialized traits. Hockey players who have superior sensory-motor, visual-spatial, body-kinesthetic and cognitive processing ability will do better on ice than players without these physiological attributes. Specific biological markers make hockey players better equipped to express higher level skills on the ice. Because of their physiological attributes, some hockey players will more easily acquire the skills needed to make them proficient hockey players. Players with good "hockey sense" have physical and cognitive advantages which allow them to understand the play and implement their skills. They "see the ice" better than their counterparts. These players "understand the play" and recognize what they must do to advantage themselves on ice. This enables the highly talented player to make better plays, score more goals, and produce better personal statistics than other players. These players have the internal biological make-up which better coordinate sensory-motor, visual-spatial, body-kinesthetic skills and the cognitive ability which allows them to process information and make quicker decisions about the direction of play when they are on the ice. This creates a superior advantage for some players and allows them to excel in the game of hockey.

Kids can be evaluated for their sensory-motor, visual-spatial and body-kinesthetic skills by psychologists, but the best indicator of these advanced skills is the player's ability to play well in their hockey games. Some players have the genetic talent which allow them to excel on ice, whereas others have limited genetic skills. Some hockey players excel in skating ability but do not have the hand-eye-stick coordination skills which increase their dexterity at making good shots on the goalie. This causes limitations which may not permit the hockey player to excel in scoring ability. The child without the natural genetic skills can still play hockey, but will struggle at scoring goals. They lack the genetic attributes which allow them to become highly skilled players. The players who lack sensory-motor, visual-spatial, body-kinesthetic and cognitive processing skills, will have to work much harder than the more genetically talented players in this sport.

Minor hockey players with the right combination of genetics will exhibit better performance on the ice. However, even young athletes who possess these innate skills do not always blossom into highly skilled hockey players. Some players may have a difficult time performing well in this sport because of other factors which impede their natural ability. For example, a player may not have the right personality (ie.temperament) for the game. John Dunn and his colleagues have shown from their research that minor hockey players whose expectations were too high and became angry when they could not accomplish a task, often failed to perform at an acceptable level on ice. This would indicate that players who are "too hard on themselves" may fail to achieve their full potential because of their "internal pessimism". This personality disposition could interfere with personal and team accomplishments.

There are many impeding factors that don't favour a player's progress in this sport. However, there are compensatory factors that still promote performance on ice. For example, a player may not have genetic talent but may have the motivation and personality needed to aspire in this sport. A hockey player with these internal skills could function well if they are hard workers on ice. Their diligence during the game could allow them to excel. There are many great athletes who play the game of hockey but not all of them have superior physiological traits. These athletes succeed in hockey because of particular personality traits that motivate them to work harder than other players. For example, tough-minded and hard-driving athletes with a motivation to win, can be instrumental in motivating other less enthusiastic players. By playing with vigour, the less skilled hockey player can serve as a role model. Their internal drive (ie. heart for the game) will inspire others to take up the challenge and also work hard. By motivating others, less skilled players encourage team-work and better output by other players.

Sport psychologists are continually searching for ways of making athletes faster and stronger in competition. Not all athletes have the genetic factors that provide them with speed on ice. Physiologists seem to agree that athletes with muscle fibre that is loaded with "fast muscle twitch" can burst quickly from a standstill position into action. Some researchers have investigated the effectiveness of exercise programs which train the muscle fibre to make "quick bursts". They have found that athletes without superior physiological traits for speed on ice can still show promise in sport if they have the right training. Kelly Lockwood and Patrick Brophey have shown that hockey players can increase their speed on ice with plyometric training. Plyometrics are exercises which foster fast and explosive ability in the athlete's muscle response (ie. fast fibril muscle twitch). These exercises train the muscles to fire quickly and thereby enhance performance of the athlete. Certain exercises, including tossing a medicine ball quickly after receiving it from a target, or leaping forward quickly from a standing long-jump position, are some of the ways of conditioning muscles to fire quickly. Certain types of exercise increase the hockey player's muscular strength. Other types of exercises, especially plyometrics, increase speed by contracting the muscles and conditioning the athlete's muscle fibres. These exercises permit the muscles to fire more rapidly and prepare the athlete for accelerated speed. This firing of muscles appears to be one of the main components found in athletes where speed and acceleration are needed to accomplish the objective of moving from one point to another quickly. Hockey players who engage in plyometric exercises will train themselves to be in a state of preparedness when acceleration is needed. This will enable the athlete to race quickly toward a puck, carry it up the ice and fire it on the net.

The hockey performance formula would indicate that young hockey players must possess a number of specific skills that enhance their behaviour. The underlying genetics mould the player's sensory-motor, visual-spatial, body-kinesthetic, and cognitive decision-making ability. Having the right genetic factors allows the young athlete the physical traits which will drive their performance on ice. Hockey performance is encouraged by a coach who ensures that the player is motivated to perform at the best of their ability. Coaches are the driving force behind the development of each player and they should know the on-ice talent of every player on their team. By knowing the strengths and weaknesses of the player, the coach can monopolize these factors to ensure that only the most highly skilled players are on the ice during highly competitive moments. It would not serve any purpose to engage players in the game of hockey who are not motivated to perform well. Strategizing by the coach can increase the motivated player's output and allow the team to maximize offensive and defensive plays. The coach ensures that the outcome of the game is driven by the performance of each player. Using those players who are highly motivated only ensures the best level of performance for the hockey team. The coach attempts to maximize the output of the team, with the anticipation that all players will work toward the same objective in the game. With this driving force behind them, hockey players increase their chance of winning in competition.

PERSONALITY TRAITS:

Talented hockey players do well in their sport because they have a combination of skills. Physiological traits are necessary in the pursuit of hockey. Other factors however, are also of some importance including the personality traits of the player. Personality is defined as the underlying traits that enhance the player's internal drive on the ice. Researchers have noted that hockey players who excel in this sport have certain characteristics that guide them to become good players. The right personality permits the hockey player to function well as a team member. These traits also assist the player in demonstrating competence on the ice. The zest for the game comes from within the player. The intrinsic need to succeed is shaped by one's personality and these internal traits influence the way the player engages in play during the hockey game.

The child who displays a personality style which consists of traits including open-mindedness, confidence, self-esteem, and poise, has some of the primary building blocks needed to become a great player. The coach can assist the youngster who possesses these traits in developing their talent. Some of the early work by Hans Eysenck showed that personality traits are genetically imprinted. A child who is "tough-minded" demonstrates a certain personality style that motivates him or her at completion of a task. This type of kid is more likely to persist in his/her attempts to win a game even though his team might be losing. The "tender-minded kid" on the other hand is more likely to give up in the same situation. This is of importance to the coach who must strive to recognize which kids on the team have the right temperament to perform under adversity. The "tough-minded" child can contend with many pressured situations whereas the "tender-minded" child will respond badly to the same situation. Stressful conditions create pressure for "tender-minded hockey players" and make them emotionally volatile. When a child is emotionally upset, he/she is less apt to think clearly and more apt to respond emotionally toward a play. When the going gets tough on the ice, the tender-minded youngster "folds under pressure of the play". A coach who is aware of the personality traits of the individual players on his team, can utilize this information to prepare a game plan. In this way, the coach has an understanding of which players are the "right fit" on the ice when the team is under pressure. Coaches realize that even in minor hockey, the right combination of players will increase the team's success. There are times when some personality styles will falter under pressured conditions. Evaluating the personality of the player can only serve to enhance the performance of the team. Kids on the hockey team who work well together, can be grouped according to their ability to function as a unit.

MOTIVATION:

Motivation is an important variable that effects a player's performance. This also drives the athlete in their on-ice activity. Psychological theorists agree that motivation and emotion co-exist and are at the basis of drive states. In his research on drive states, Robert Beck noted that when behaviour is reinforced it serves to enhance motivational output.

In minor hockey, players don't receive money for their performance but they do receive praise from the coach. Hockey players can attain recognition from the coach for individual effort and team cooperation. The implication would be that by working hard in the game and achieving goals, assists, and wins, the player will receive praise and recognition. As the season progresses, the hockey player achieves status with his team statistics. The player learns that winning creates positive emotional states (ie. feeling good about one's performance). Hockey players achieve more satisfaction from positive experiences. Thus, they work harder to win games, because this is a more powerful reward than losing the game. Activities which are positive experiences are generally perceived by young players as being more rewarding. They value positive experiences and perceive them to be of merit.

It is difficult for a hockey parent to increase a child's interest toward an activity. One cannot force a child to take an interest in hockey if they don't like the sport. Kids who don't have fun in hockey will never do well at this sport. They lack the interest in performing well because they don't view it as a positive experience. Children who are forced to play hockey will go through the motions but will never have the "heart" (motivation /interest) for the game. Without the "heart" to play hockey, a child will never perform at 100 % output. Parents can't teach a child motivation in hockey, this is a drive state that comes from within the child.

Hockey parents must understand the guiding principles of motivation and use these to improve their child's performance. Research by S. Wuerth and colleagues found that parents offer different directives to their children in sports. Mothers tend to be a source of praise and understanding for their child, whereas fathers tend to espouse goal orientation for the child. By encouraging and providing direction, parents can be instrumental in increasing their child's performance. When the emotional support, objectives or goal orientation are missing, the coach must provide this input. The external rewards (ie. praise) and internal rewards (ie. feeling good about personal accomplishment) must be properly conditioned in the child. They will allow the child to feel good about their on-ice performance.

INCENTIVES:

The last variable in the hockey performance formula is incentive. This refers to the reward a child obtains for engaging in the activity. Those involved in "big league hockey" make handsome salaries for playing the sport. Minor hockey players will never be paid for their involvement in this sport. Children play this sport because they value the intrinsic reward of this fun-filled activity. Children involve themselves in hockey because of its tempo, skill development and the friendships they acquire during this experience. Youngsters who have a genuine interest in hockey don't need money to play this sport. Praise and recognition appear to be the important reinforcers of their behaviour. Although tangible rewards (ie. ribbons, medals) are not required by young hockey players, many kids do benefit from these external reinforcers. Some players are sufficiently motivated by the intrinsic rewards (ie. good feeling from making a play or scoring a goal) because these propel young athletes to engage in this sport. Intrinsic rewards have been defined as the internal motivators that create the "good feelings" for one's performance in the game.

Hockey parents need to become aware of the external and internal motivators that inspire their children. When my first son commenced hockey he was highly influenced by external reinforcers. Praise, a hot chocolate, and his name appearing in the sports news of the local newspaper, were motivators that highly influenced his game. He had a need for external rewards because they provided him with the feedback necessary to encourage his game performance. Some 10 years later my younger son has commenced minor hockey. This younger lad does not require external rewards to perform well on the ice. His performance is encouraged by the positive feelings that come from making a pass or stopping an opponent from scoring. He is pleased when he receives an award (ie. hustler of the game or MVP) but external rewards are not the primary factors that motivate his performance.

Children vary in their need for reinforcement. Some parents tell me they use money to encourage their child to play hockey. This may not be the best way to reward a child, even though it seems to work for some kids and for some parents. Money appears to be a motivator for NHL players so why shouldn't it be good for minor hockey players? If hockey parents use money as a reinforcer to increase a child's motivation, they must ensure they use the same payoff for scoring assists as they do for making goals. In this way, the parent does not encourage the child to only want to score goals. Encouraging one activity (ie. scoring goals) over the other (ie. scoring assists) will advocate to the child that hockey is not a team sport. The parent must always remember that hockey is a team sport that encourages cooperation. Hockey players can aptly respond to this demand by assisting others to score goals and this is in line with the cooperation that comes with this team sport.

Children value certain rewards. Praise, hot chocolate, candy or money may be suitable reinforcers for your child. Hockey parents must attempt to understand what propels their child's behaviour and use these reinforcers to encourage performance on the ice. Children involved in hockey may benefit from extrinsic rewards especially when they first commence playing the game. But after a period of time, children may satiate from the external rewards and come to realize they are also motivated by intrinsic rewards. Minor hockey players learn that personal accomplishments are more important than the external rewards received for these accomplishments.

Behavioural psychologist B.F. Skinner, believed that behaviour could be increased in a positive direction if rewards (reinforcers) were provided. Extrinsic rewards (praise, money) encourage a child to play hockey because of the outcome derived from these external rewards. If the child doesn't play hard, he or she will not get any rewards. These extrinsic rewards however, are not necessary for all children. Some children enjoy playing hockey because of the good feelings they obtain from playing the game. Some children play the game of hockey because they obtain both the extrinsic and intrinsic rewards. Other children may play hockey because it is a fun-filled activity; these children enjoy playing hockey because of the conditioned associations (ie. fun) the game provides. A child doesn't have to be outstanding at hockey to obtain enjoyment from this sport. As they become proficient at the game, they feel good about their progress. Parents and coaches praise kids because of their acquired skills and their performance on ice. The child reaps the rewards for their performance; they receive ribbons or trophies (positive reinforcers) and after winning championships have their team picture printed in the local newspapers. These reinforcers appear to be some of the best motivators and inspire minor hockey players to do their best at the sport.

Hockey parents must understand that reinforcers can create some conflict if they are not accurately delivered. During the process of administering these rewards, the wrong message can be instilled in young players. Condoning certain behaviour with praise or money may only encourage performing an activity to receive a payoff. The child may learn that personal achievement is dependent upon receiving some reward. This could be problematic because a player's interest in pursuing hockey would only be encouraged by extrinsic rewards. These reinforcers might override the true reason for playing the game and come to interfere with the intrinsic motivators. Love of hockey should come from within the child and not from the external rewards bestowed by the parent.

Over the ten years that I have been involved in minor hockey, I have observed that some parents use extrinsic rewards too frequently. It would seem the child's hockey performance is often controlled by these external rewards. After the game, I have heard minor hockey players demanding large sums of money from their parents for their performance. Parents who offer their child money for every goal scored, can create problems for the child. When monetary value is attached to hockey performance it only serves to encourage these extrinsic rewards. The hockey parent must remember that young hockey players between the age of 6 and 12 are at the concrete stage of development. According to Jean Piaget, children think inductively at the concrete stage, which means they do not have sophisticated reasoning skills to evaluate information. By virtue of these limited reasoning skills, the child learns they can obtain a larger amount of money for scoring a goal and a diminutive amount of money or no money for making an assist. In their minds they inductively reason that goals must be more valuable than assists. Invariably the child learns to infer that hockey performance is determined by extrinsic rewards (ie. money) and that certain accomplishments like scoring goals is more important than making assists. Although the hockey parent's intentions were admirable, they have unintentionally shaped up behaviour which is against the grain of cooperation and teammanship which is necessary in hockey. What transpires in this situation is a young hockey player who is motivated only to score goals and the evolution of the proverbial "puck hog". No one likes a puck hog on their team; this type of player does not share the play or the puck with other players. Engaging in the selfish act of not passing the puck only confirms this players lack of teammanship.

According to Jean Piaget, children from about the age of 2 until age 6 function at the preoperational stage of development. They engage in ego-centric behaviour. During this period, children are self-focused and self-centred. They perceive the world as a place where their needs should come before any other person's needs. This way of behaving has self-preservation value because it guarantees their needs will be met. By the time the child attains age 6 however, they start moving away from their ego-centric focus. Through interaction with others, children begin to recognize the value of playing and sharing with other children. Parents reinforce this attitude in family settings and express their dismay when the child does not share with other siblings. In this way, the child learns cooperation in relationships and engages in sharing with their peers. By encouraging this process the child learns to get along with others and learns to fit into society. The transition in the thinking process from inductive to deductive reasoning, which occurs at about age 6 to 12 allows the child to recognize the value of sharing and assists in their development of friendships and team cooperation.

Hockey parents who only encourage "goal scoring" through the use of monetary rewards, reinforce self-centred activity in their child. By this act, hockey parents discourage personal growth of children by not allowing them to share with others. This self-focused approach only influences the personal ego-focused striving of children. At age 6, when the child should be learning to share and learning to become a team player, they begin a journey of self centredness and are only interested in their own pursuits. Hockey parents need to understand that they are highly influential and can have an effect on their children's behaviour. The parent needs to reflect on their use of reinforcement, because it could have significant negative impact on the child. In their over zealous attempt to get their child interested in the sport of hockey, some parents may be encouraging the wrong type of behaviour. Some parents shape up behaviours that are against the grain of cooperation and fair play. Cooperation with others is a preliminary attribute for team-work and this is paramount to the success of a team. In hockey, the main focus is attempting to get the team to function as a unit. Parents have to ensure their use of reinforcement does not exclude this concept.

Children who play the game of hockey have different personalities. They also have different reasons for their interest in this activity. Providing motivators that lead to outcome (ie. goals, assists, trophies) only assist the child in learning the extrinsic rewards of the game. True motivation to play hockey comes from the internal rewards. There is a general notion held by hockey parents that children who do well at this activity have "heart" for the game. This infers that children who truly love the game of hockey put forth their best effort because they want to do well. Good performance creates good feelings and the development of positive self-worth in the child.

If a hockey parent wants the child to perform at his/her highest level, then a number of factors have to be included in the child's performance behaviour. Hockey parents should insist that children work on all aspects of their game in order to perform at a high level. Hockey parents should never expect young players to be motivated only by external rewards. True gamesmanship arises from learning the skills and showing motivation to play the game. Youngsters must appreciate the basis of the intrinsic and extrinsic rewards they receive for their performance. Hockey is not always about winning but about having fun and developing skills. These combined factors enhance the child's self-esteem (ie. positive worth). Playing hockey will allow the child to learn a number of skills including listening to directives given by the coach and learning ways of cooperating with others.

Children need to use their cognitive skills in their processing of information. Some of these cognitive skills are not always available at an early age because the brain is not fully mature. Although sensory-motor skill development commences in the first two years of life, it isn't until approximately 20 years of age, that the brain has fully developed. A child shows much growth in the first 15 years of life and it is during this time of physical development that many of the hockey skills are laid into a pattern. By age 15, most hockey kids are either proficient at the skills required to further their involvement in upper-level hockey, or they come to realize they have reached their pinnacle of success. Many will play this sport long after minor hockey has finished. There are few hockey players who have the skills needed to progress to the Junior, University or Provincial/State levels. Many kids have the motivation needed in this sport but don't have high-level skills. These minor hockey players should not be dismayed. The chance of making it to big league hockey is possible, but not always probable. Once they have completed minor hockey, the skilled athlete can join the ranks of those players who become involved in "pick up" hockey leagues. They can play hockey into their senior years and engage in camaraderie with fellow players.

A CHILD'S EVALUATION OF SKILLS:

I believe that it is important for youngsters to have the ability to motivate themselves. Behavioural charting sometimes assists the child. This is useful because it provides a concrete model in which the child/adolescent can evaluate their skills and objectives. In Appendix 1 & Appendix 2, I have compiled a Hockey Player Self-Evaluation Chart and a Goalie Self-Evaluation Chart. An overview of these charts will allow the player/goalie to rate themselves on a number of skills prior to the game and following the game. By taking the time to do this pre-game and post-game, youngsters can provide themselves with feedback regarding their game performance. The child might also find it useful to get feedback from the coach by having him/her use these evaluation charts following the game. This will provide two separate perspectives and maintain some external reliability regarding the child's game performance. Players sometimes tend to be too lenient in their evaluation of their game activity and at other times they may be too critical. With input from the coach, the player would have more accurate knowledge of their activity on ice.

CHAPTER SIX

AGGRESSION IN THE ARENA
PARENTS ON THE HOT PLATE:

There have been many incidents of parents who have lost control of their emotions while they were at the arena. According to the media, the aggressive behaviour exhibited by these parents was entirely out of character for them. When hockey parents respond in a violent manner, many become concerned. One can only wonder what factors influenced these emotional outbursts. There are mitigating circumstances to every violent reaction and often times one has to examine the underlying biological or situational events which led to these incidents.

The criminal trial involving Thomas Junta, a hockey father convicted of involuntary manslaughter, provides us with some insight to the complexity of violence. Ostensibly Thomas Junta, a 44 year old hockey parent was found guilty of involuntary manslaughter against Michael Costin, a 40 year old coach and hockey father. Information documented on this case reported that Mr. Junta was sentenced to 6 to 10 years for the fatal beating of Coach Costin. According to the media and court reports, an argument had taken place between these men because of "rough play" during a practise. Following an argument, Mr. Junta and Coach Costin were involved in a physical altercation. Initially, an employee at the Burbank arena had to intervene and was able to stop the altercation. Coach Costin returned to the dressing room but shortly thereafter went to the arena lobby where he encountered Thomas Junta. A scuffle broke out between the men and some physical blows delivered by Thomas Junta ruptured an artery in Michael Costin's neck leading to a brain hemorrhage. The coach was taken to a local hospital but succumbed to his injury a day later.

At his trial, the court deemed this was not a premeditated act and consequently Thomas Junta was convicted of a lesser charge of involuntary manslaughter. The tragedy of this case was not only the death of Coach Costin and criminal conviction of Thomas Junta but the fact that hockey kids and parents at the Burbank Ice Arena in Reading, Massachusetts had witnessed this traumatic event. The disconcerting aspect of the Junta and Costin matter was the fact that both men's children were members of the same minor hockey team. During the court proceedings these men were described by friends as caring parents who attended to the needs of their children. There was some discussion in court of historical fact pertaining to personal difficulties each man had faced in the past. At the time of the violent incident however, both men appeared to be stable parents attempting to nurture and provide for their children's welfare.

Parents are concerned when acts of aggression occur in the community. Members of the community become quite distraught when hockey parents lose control of their emotions, fly into a rage and attempt injury on one another. The incident that occurred between Thomas Junta and Michael Costin is one that could happen to any parent. Given a situation that is fraught with tension and frustration, emotions escalate and lead to violent behaviour. In my profession, I have encountered many adult inmates in maximum security jails. Some of these offenders have been incarcerated on manslaughter convictions because they inadvertently killed another person in a fight.

These inmates had not premeditated the act of homicide but accidentally killed their victims in the process of a physical altercation. Any behavioural situation which escalates to violence can lead to serious consequences for those who become involved.

Anger is an emotion which is released from a physiological structure buried deep in the brain. Aggression is the hostile reaction that emerges when anger becomes charged and can no longer be controlled by cerebral mechanisms. When aggression is externalized toward others it can lead to violence, physical injury or death. Within each human is a potential aggressive beast. Its venom lies quietly, but on occasion can surface to spawn its rage and vengeance. Even those with the best of inhibitory mechanisms can loose control of this beast. Given the proper conditions, including the biological state of the host and the situational circumstances, aggression can become uncontrollable. It is during these periods that hostility rages full of sound and fury waging its violence on those who would scorn it.

There have been many incidents of hockey violence reported by the media. It is important to evaluate the causative agents because this will allow us to understand the caustic events that precipitate these violent incidents. Only then will we begin to comprehend ways of harnessing anger which can lead to aggressive acts. There isn't any reasonable argument to support the use of aggression, except of course in the case of self-defense when one's life is threatened. When aggression flares in the hockey arena, it creates a frightening dilemma. Although homicide is infrequent, the incidents of aggression in the arena have increased over the past decade. The gravity of these incidents have caused much concern to those involved in this sport. An evaluation of the mitigating circumstances which precipitate aggression and violence must be examined to understand the causal mechanisms. Behaviour is influenced by myriad variables but the ultimate act of violence is rarely exhibited. In society, most members act in accordance with prescribed rules. According to those who have researched dangerousness, less than one percent of the populace are deemed to be dangerous homicidal psychopaths intent on maliciously injuring others.

There are many precursors which lead to aggressive behaviour. One would have to examine these to come to some conclusion regarding the factors that precipitate violence in the hockey arena. Generally, hockey parents who take their children to arenas are perceived as nurturing and caring types. They are interested in activities which will allow their children to develop skills and benefit from exercise found in this sport. There are some hockey parents, who create excessive demands and expect their children will aspire to NHL stardom. In the process of pressuring their children to achieve this objective, these parents become enmeshed in a vicarious personal struggle to have their child excel in a sport in which they may have personally failed. This creates conflict for themselves and places pressure on their children. Unable to achieve the ice-time they believe is required for their child to develop the skills necessary for success, some parents become frustrated and express anger. For these hockey parents, venting their emotions can lead to the use of excessive aggressive behaviour. It is during these episodes that some hockey parents allow their anger to take control of them; and after the act of aggression, the parent expresses embarrassment at their behaviour. Some assaultive parents appear confused by the incident and maintain they had "blacked out" during the episode. It is during this brief moment that emotions raged and violence erupted.

Typically one believes that parents who enrol their kids in hockey are reasonable and stable people. They present as pleasant, good natured, community citizens who are concerned with the welfare of their young. The news of a hockey parent losing control and running amok in some raging manner raises eyebrows in the community. What emerges from these media reports are feelings juxtaposed between reality and surrealism. Leon Festinger, a social psychologist believed that people attempt to achieve consistency in their behaviour. The idea of hockey parents displaying nurturing qualities for their children by involving them in sports, is incongruent with the notion of an aggressive raging hockey parent assaulting others at the arena. These incidents create confusion and ire in the public domain. The populace become concerned and demand an explanation when hockey parents lose control of their behaviour and exhibit random acts of violence. There have been recent media reports describing parental aggression in the arena. Listed below are a few of these incidents. In some instances the perpetrators were banned from the arena and at other times had to attend court to answer to the charges:

1) "Hockey dad charged with assaulting daughter":—a parent grabs his daughter's face mask, screams and shakes her.
2) "Parents must sign behavioural contract before their child is allowed to play hockey":—parental aggression in the hockey arena lead officials to seek measures that would ban them for offensive behaviour.
3) "Parent aims laser at the eyes of his daughter's opponents".
4) "Hockey moms begin brawl in a locker room".
5) "Parent assaults his son's opponent".
6) "Spectators yell verbal abuse at opponent players".
7) "Hockey father chokes the coach".

These examples are only a few of the media reports in which parents have lost emotional control and engaged in aggressive behaviour. People can be inspired by their feelings and at other times fall victim to loss of control of their emotions. When parents lose their ability to think clearly and respond aggressively, society becomes concerned. Adults have fully formed cognitive abilities which allow them to appreciate the nature and quality of their actions and to make proper decisions. With an intact cerebral cortex, a parent should have the capacity to think, plan and behave in an acceptable and socially sanctioned manner. The only time that a person should act aggressively is in an instance of self-defense, or when there is a loss of behavioural control, because of a brain impairment caused by disease or accident.

Hockey arenas were built for people. These public centres provide citizens with a community resource where they can engage in activity and have fun. When people gather in arenas, the "stress" created by every day pressures should subside as one enters the doors. Problems arise however, when individuals bring their complex personal problems to the arenas. Sometimes, parents cannot enjoy the game of hockey because they are too busy worrying about their child's advancement in this sport. They become easily frustrated and perplexed by the least complex of situations. For these parents the amount of ice-time their child gets becomes an issue of paramount importance. One verbally aggressive parent reiterated that he paid the same hockey registration fee as other parents therefore his kid should have access to equal playing-time. This is a valid argument and the premise of fair ice-time should be encouraged in hockey leagues. The reality however, is that some coaches violate the child's right to receive fair ice-time. This is usually done to enable the coach to develop a highly competitive hockey team. Much to the chagrin of many, this action creates frustration for the parent and the child who plays hockey. Situations which are perceived as frustrating for the parent can lead to acts of verbal and physical aggression. These situations are breeding grounds of discontent and often cause imminent diaster. The violent incidents that arise because of these pressures are often spontaneous and unpremeditated by parents. When a volatile parent explodes, a spontaneous blow to someone's head or a fall on a hard object is all that is required to cause bodily injury or death to its victim.

There are other explanations for aggression in hockey arenas. Some hockey parents take the outcome of the game personally. These highly driven and achievement oriented people believe their child should win every game. These parents do their outmost to pressure children into winning at all costs. Aggression is expressed by parents as they "coach" their child behind the scenes. Hockey parents harangue their children into using every method to thwart their opponents. Parents can be heard on the sideline encouraging their kids to "hit and injure" players to ensure a win. It is the parent's belief that aggression is an important component of hockey and should be used as an ancillary measure to win the game.

Children are malleable and come to believe the verbal ranting of the parent. At other times they merely adhere to the parent's ideologies to cease the endless banter. Often times, the aggression the parent teaches behind the scenes is merely a reflection of the parent's own displaced aggressive feelings. Parents who live vicariously through their children have not been able to achieve their own goals in hockey. Consequently these parents motivate their child to become high achievers in order to satisfy the parent's personal needs.

The parent who espouses aggression on the ice can often be found socially exchanging information with other hockey parents who uphold similar views. The aggression which these parents harbour is displayed in their negative banter and rumour mongering. The negative ramifications of this behaviour is particulary problematic when parents express these openly aggressive and hostile views toward others. This type of activity causes emotional reactivity and aggressive behaviour is discharged. According to social psychologists, these situations can often lead to mob activity. When this occurs in the arena, it creates tension for referees who must control on-ice activity and contend with the bantering of the aggressive crowd.

Social aggression can be observed at any given time in arenas. The smallest of events can set off the crowd. At other times, it is merely the expression of aggression by one member which incites the crowd into frenzied activity. The outcome of this situation is usually a function of the level of emotionality of the crowd and their ability/inability to inhibit their anger. I can recall an incident when I attended a hockey game in a remote northern community. It was the last round of the regular season games. The opponent team was in last place in a league of 5 teams. This team was vying for a win which could place them in fourth position and allow them to advance to the quarter-finals. One could understand the team's level of emotional arousal, as the players skated diligently in their concerted effort to win the game. The atmosphere at the arena was charged with volatile energy. The parents from the opponent team naturally wanted their kids to win and attempted to bolster the on-ice activity with their loud tempo which filtered through the building. The first game was played well by both teams but the game ended with a 6-4 score, in favour of the visitors.

A second game took place later that evening between the same teams. The mood of some parents had changed and could only be described as emotionally tense. Parents seated and those standing behind the glass, were shouting at their team to score at all costs. A deluge of comments which included "hit them" and "destroy them" were screamed in unison by the agitated spectators. Being of larger stature, the opponent players used physical contact to stop many of the skilled plays. A parent from the opponent team blurted out that physical contact was a part of the game and if the other team couldn't take it, they should pack their bags and go home. At this particular point, the atmosphere of the arena was filled with aggressive overtones and rife for mob activity. The opponent team was losing badly and the chance of winning the game was quickly slipping from their grasp. Without the win, they would not advance and the regular hockey season would be over for this team. Two parents could be heard in the crowd verbally insulting one another. Negative expletives were fired in both directions. I stood in silence and wondered whether the out of control behaviour would escalate to a physical altercation. Rather than attempting to calm themselves, these parents continued to threaten one another with violence and injury. If it had not been for the intervention of some "emotionally calm" parents, an altercation would certainly have taken place that evening.

After the game finished, the crowd slowly departed without any physical altercation. Two burly police officers stood nearby fixing their cold stares on the spectators as they shuffled their way into the winter evening. An occasional comment of discontent was muttered by the crowd as they filed from the building. The anger which had emerged during the game had been controlled. The presence of the police officers had ensured that no violence took place that evening. Leaving the building was a welcomed contrast to the environment of the arena, heated by caustic comments of the unruly crowd.

The aggression that had raged inside the building had been contained. It would however, continue to rear its head at other games. Emotions often erupt in spectators who lose their focus. The volatility of the crowd is usually marked by tension and the verbalization of angry feelings. Often times, spectators become enmeshed in the banter. Those who are emotionally aroused become volatile and lose control of their behaviour often acting in a way which is out of character for them.

Later that evening, the parents assembled in the hospitality room at the motel. We discussed the game and the tension that permeated the event. Some parents expressed astonishment over the hostile mood which had prevailed. Others merely shrugged their shoulders stating this was reflective of the hockey environment. Social psychologists have stated that when people are involved in an emotionally charged situation, they are apprehensive because of the threat of personal violence. At the hockey game that evening however, some parents had intervened and calmed the spectators who had threatened assault on one another. Bystander intervention had eliminated the probability of aggression and the presence of the police officers had also calmed the mood of the crowd.

Later that evening, I interacted with the hockey dad who had been involved in the aggressive incident at the arena. He informed me that when he was a youngster, his hockey team and accompanying parents often had to fight their way out of arenas, especially when they won at out of town competitive games. Although this parent didn't present as overly hostile, he agreed that being pressured and tantalized by others had led him to lose control of his emotions. Apparently when he became angry, he would lose his ability to think straight and this would heighten his aggressive nature. It was his feeling that if he had become involved in a fight at the arena, he would have been charged and landed in jail for the evening.

Humans vary in their innate aggressive behaviour. There are differences between males and females with the former gender exhibiting more aggression. There are also individual differences within the male species with some males having

higher levels of aggressive display because of elevated testos-
terone levels. Some individuals are naturally more impulsive
and this leads to spontaneous acts of aggression. The intensity
of an external stressor can fuel the emotional energy which
leads to violent urges. It is in these situations that parents have
to be capable of controlling their underlying anger, before it
escalates and creates hostile or violent behaviour. Social psychologists Bib Latane and James Darley would argue that in a
situation where aggression emerges, some people are less apt to
get involved because of fear of being harmed. In the situation
described above however, hockey parents had intervened to
diffuse the hostile behaviour.

AGGRESSION IN HOCKEY PLAYERS:

Many believe that physical contact is an important component
of the game of hockey. It is known in the hockey world that by
using physical aggression, one can interfere with an opponent's
ability to complete a play. The more that one hinders the opponent through body-checking, the greater the likelihood of a
reduction in scoring. Generally, it is thought that the best way
to take an opponent out of play is through the use of physical
body contact or by slamming the opponent against the boards.
Hockey Canada's New Standards of Play does not condone assaultive activity nor physical contact which can lead to injury.

Some coaches in minor hockey believe that children who
learn physical contact at an earlier age will be less likely to
experience an injury during a hockey game. The impact of
body-checking at an early age however, has been investigated
by many researchers and the results show that body checking does indeed cause serious injury to young hockey players. James King and Claire Leblanc found that boys between
the ages of 10 to 13, who were allowed to body-check, had a

greater incidence of injury than players from leagues where body-checking was not allowed. Furthermore, King and Leblanc also found that adolescent boys 14 years of age and older, who had learned to use body-checking at an earlier age, also had more injuries than boys who had not engaged in this activity at an earlier age. These results are consistent with the findings of other investigators who imply that physical contact in young hockey players is not of any benefit. The data show that body-checking renders injuries to players by causing brain, spinal cord and/or body impairment.

There seems to be a prevailing attitude regarding aggression in hockey. Aggressive players in minor hockey are being castigated for their role in body-checking because of the physical damage experienced by its victims. Physical contact leads to body injury and interferes with a player's game of hockey. Furthermore, there are ramifications including possible civil and criminal litigious procedures. The outcome of these situations is often dependent upon the gravity of the offensive behaviour which caused the injury. If precedents are set in court proceedings, players, parents and officials will want to re-evaluate aggressive behaviour and physical contact on the ice. Most parents find hockey a time consuming and expensive sport. If they have to start purchasing liability insurance because of subsequent injury, they may consider placing their children in other less aggressive sports. The gravity of the physical contact leading to injury is becoming of greater consequence to the perpetrator. If the act is considered to have been hostile or retaliatory in nature and the victim is seriously injured, there can be some long-term consequences for the offender. These sanctions can range from minor penalties to expulsion from the game. In recent cases in minor hockey, some players were expelled for many games or the entire season because of their infraction.

In our communities, aggression is not tolerated. Sanctions are imposed against perpetrators who behave aggressively and the Criminal Justice System deems assault as an indictable offense, with serious consequences for the perpetrator. In society we are taught to avoid aggressive actions. If one uses aggression as a response to a situation, there is a high probability the individual will be labelled as an "aggressor" or "bully". Hockey players and parents are forced to leave arenas when they behave aggressively. In certain cases, some perpetrators are criminally charged and convicted for their actions. At one time in hockey, it seemed that one could engage in aggressive acts and perpetrators were not incriminated because of their actions. More recently however, aggression isn't tolerated as it had been in the past. Hockey officials do not condone this type of behaviour and hockey associations are currently attempting to regain control of behaviour in the arena by sanctioning actions of those who engage in aggressive acts. Although aggression is tolerated to a certain degree in hockey, by displaying too much aggressive behaviour on ice is not tolerated by the Minor Hockey Associations. Players who aggress beyond what is deemed acceptable are now being chastised, given fines and ostracized from the game of hockey. Individuals who behave aggressively in arenas are not only required to leave but are often required to undertake emotion control programs (ie. anger management) before they are allowed access to hockey games.

Concerns have arisen in minor hockey associations because of violent behaviour in the arenas. Many ask "what level of aggression is acceptable and what degree of physical contact is tolerated?" Should the consequences for the child who physically assaults another player leading to an injury be any different than the consequences for the kid who engages in a serious assault rendering his opponent a long-term injury? If one considers these situations, it becomes obvious that acts of aggression vary in their gravity. Hockey players who exhibit aggression on the ice will sometimes indicate they were not aware of the seriousness of the act at the time of its occurrence. Some players believe they were acting in accordance with the rules of hockey. One must question whether aggression resulted because of the players' lack of comprehension of the rules of hockey or because of the players' heightened emotionality and their inability to inhibit their emotions at the time of the offense.

Players are required to engage in proper reasoning during the game, even if they are emotionally charged. Some would argue however, that its difficult for the hockey player to think rationally when they are emotionally aroused. Some players in minor hockey indicate they feel justified when they exhibit retaliatory behaviour after being hit by an opponent. Reasoning, planning and decision-making take place in the frontal cortex of the brain. Research by Sidney Segalowicz and Patricia Davies would indicate that the frontal cortex is not fully developed until one is a young adult. Poor decisions by minor hockey players may at times be due to this cognitive immaturity rather than some premeditated action to harm another person. Young players may not fully appreciate the nature and consequences of their actions when they engage in aggressive actions on the ice.

Seldom do hockey players premeditate a wilful act of violence against another hockey player. In some cases it is merely a "reflex like action" which leads to an act of aggression. In other instances, the player has been assigned to a team because of their aggressive nature. Hockey players who are perceived as "enforcers" are generally avoided by most players who fear injury from these aggressors. The concept of enforcers was a common phenomenon in NHL hockey during the 1980's. Jill

LeClair has noted from her research, that during the 1980's highly aggressive players signed contracts not because of their skills but because of their ability to deliver physical punishment to their opponents. Enforcers are rarely seen in minor hockey, because the game has evolved into an sport where skill is used to defeat opponents and the rules and standards of play enforced by referees.

The notion of aggressive behaviour has led to much research in this area as investigators attempt to understand the complexity of this issue. According to researchers there are three types of expressed aggression in society. They are defined as follows:

1) Innate aggression—the type of aggression an individual possesses because of genetic factors. Physical energy is released depending on the level of anger and the stimulus.

2) Situational aggression—this type of aggression results from frustration. This is consistent with the research of psychologists who believe that a person frustrated by an event or person responds aggressively toward the source of frustration.

3) Vicarious or modelled aggression—this notion of aggression is consistent with aggressive responding after one views others engaged in a similar display of this behaviour.

Whatever the basis of aggression in hockey, the outcome will lead to some physical injury. Research by behavioral scientists would indicate that individuals who are assaulted will generally respond with aggression. Antagonized hockey players respond in accordance with their level of innate aggression and their perception of behaviour displayed by the aggressor. To reduce levels of aggression in young hockey players, it is important for the coach to downplay physical violence on the ice. Some researchers believe that one of the best ways of reducing aggression is by not reinforcing this behaviour when it occurs. John Dunn and his colleagues believe that it is better for the coach in minor hockey, to only condone a player's skills and competence on the ice rather than the outcome of the game. An example of this is the hockey coach who expresses the notion "you guys really worked hard during the game" versus "you guys lost the game for us". In this way, the coach takes the pressure off the kid and does not reinforce their feelings of frustration and anger for loss of the game. Players tend to be highly charged during a hockey game. When they do not accomplish their expected goals they become angry. This can often lead to aggression, especially when the player is frustrated and their expectancies have not reached fruition.

Some coaches have indicated that aggression has always been an expected component in hockey. They believe it is a necessary ritual that has become part of the game. An article that appeared in Roy MacGregor's column "This Country" noted that "76 percent of true hockey fans don't want fighting eliminated in hockey". Since its inception, physical aggression was permitted in hockey. Players were expected to use physical contact to stop their opponents from scoring. Mr. MacGregor, columnist for the Globe and Mail, is quick to point out that aggression at the NHL level, especially hits to the head, will only lead to serious injury and possible death to the player.

Some coaches take a diametrically opposite stance regarding aggression. They perceive hockey as a sport requiring skills, ability and positive outcomes (ie.fun and winning). The game of hockey was never developed as a sport of physical aggression. Hockey parents are cognizant of the finesse of this sport and have generally had the opportunity to view hockey at the olympic, national and junior levels. It is at this level of hockey that one begins to realize the importance of skill and ability.

Good competition between opponent teams is about play-making, sportsmanship and winning. Competition on ice has never been about violence, aggression or injury.

Recently, the notion of physical aggression in sport has begun its downward spiral. Minor hockey players have been cautioned of their use of physical contact during the game. They are being told that any attempt to annihilate one's opponents through physical injury will result in minor and major penalty infractions. Engaging in aggression during minor hockey games has lead to immediate expulsion of the player. Penalties for infractions can vary depending on the gravity of the offense, the contact made and the degree of injury.

In many sporting activities, there is a certain level of overt aggression. Spectators seem to respond favourably to those who lose control and exhibit hostile behaviour. The aggressive display of the tennis player who jumps up and down and smashes his racket because of a bad game, or the golfer angered by a poor round who smashes his club into the trunk of a tree, are some examples of situations which provoke a smile on a spectator's face. Situations where violence is directed toward others however, are not looked on with favour. When athletes are purposely injured or spectators victimized, these situations create concerns for sporting associations. Soccer fans rioting and engaging in violent mob activity are scorned because of their abhorrent actions. Their assaults on others and damage to property are of little benefit to the sport. Hockey players who threaten and abuse opposing teams are also viewed with contempt. Their loss of emotional control is not well tolerated by the public or the officials. There are many situations of aggression and violence in society. These would indicate that human beings are not very good at controlling their emotions. Once an emotion of anger is aroused, it is difficult to channel into a socially approved or less offensive behaviour. It appears that energized anger can only lead to a discharge of aggression which often times leads to violent consequences.

Physical contact has been ingrained in the game of hockey. The level of aggression expressed, is however of concern to parents. Hockey parents must ensure their child is aware of the consequences of aggression. If the hockey parent can make children cognizant of the detrimental impact of injury, it will assist the child in reflecting on their actions on the ice. Players in minor hockey must learn to use their reasoning skills, to inhibit impulsive feelings. Constant feedback is needed from the coach during the game so the players' actions are properly controlled. Parents can influence the child's reasoning and behaviour to ensure their judgement is consistent with socially sanctioned mores. Parents who are not aware of the techniques to control the child's behaviour can undertake courses which would teach them these skills. Apparently this form of educational component has commenced in many cities and parents are expected to demonstrate acceptable behaviour while they attend sporting events.

PHYSICAL CONTACT AND INJURY:

When kids first commence hockey at the Tyke development level, there is little evidence of aggression on the ice. Over the ten year period of my involvement in minor hockey, I can only recall one incident in Tyke development where a player aggressed toward an opponent. In this situation, a goalie was unhappy with a goal scored against him. The seven year old retaliated by hitting the opponent player on the helmet with his stick. The goalie was immediately chastised and spent some time in the penalty box. This situation likely taught him that aggressive infractions would not be tolerated in the game of hockey.

Generally, players are too busy learning the game of hockey to initiate an aggressive act against another child. Parents at the Tyke level are seldom heard uttering remarks of injury against young hockey players. Most parents of Tyke development players are too busy admiring the hockey plays and less apt to express negative comments toward players. Essentially, parents at this level are more interested in stick handling and goal scoring and less interested in verbal aggression. After the game, parents are busy giving their children "high fives" and telling them what a great game they had. Hockey parents at the Tyke development level of hockey don't seem to express violent intentions. This attitude however, changes in parents at some point from Tyke development to Midget level hockey. It would seem that personal and social factors influence the release of anger and this is exhibited in the aggressive remarks made by parents.

When a child commences competitive hockey there is a need to achieve success. When this is not accomplished, frustration usually occurs. To compound this problem, as kids get older they become involved in high level leagues that permit physical contact with other players. Coaches and parents seem to advocate the use of physical contact as an accepted practice for their children. Physical contact is used to control the play and thwart opponents from winning the game. Skilled hockey players become a threat to the goalie and to hinder these players from scoring a goal, physical aggression becomes a paramount part of the game. Parents are often heard in the arena yelling "hit that kid, take him down" or "go for the body". At this stage, minor hockey becomes a contact sport which is oriented toward physical aggression. By using physical force, opponents are prevented from scoring goals. Physical aggression becomes tolerated and accepted as a part of the game.

Medical professionals have expressed their concern about aggression in hockey because of the injuries that prevail from physical contact. Some coaches favour the delivery of body-checks in hockey, arguing that it is advantageous for the child to commence this at an earlier age. These coaches believe there is a lower likelihood of injury at an earlier age because youngsters are smaller in stature and have less body weight. By learning the basics of physical contact at an early age, some coaches believe that minor hockey players will learn techniques which are in compliance with the regulations established by Hockey Canada. Furthermore, proponents of physical contact believe that younger kids need to learn body-checking to ensure they have this skill when they reach the higher levels of hockey. Many who advocate this approach surmise the gravity of injury will be less serious at a younger age.

After a child achieves pubescence, hormonal changes in the body augment the child's physical growth and strengthens their musculature. Cognition also accelerates during adolescence. Research by Jean Piaget has indicated that adolescents, having reached a formal stage of cognitive growth, show improved reasoning skills. The advancement in cognitive ability allows the adolescent hockey player to make better decisions about hockey plays. Having knowledge of the "rules of physical contact", the adolescent may be less apt to engage in a hit which could lead to serious injury of their opponents.

Those who oppose physical contact argue that children should wait until they are older, so they can learn ways of avoiding injury. Parents have to be aware of the dangers of physical contact because injury can leave a youngster permanently disabled. Parents have to understand that the impact of body injury can have debilitating consequences to the youngster's brain, spinal cord and body. Hockey parents have to be aware of the implications of injury before they allow their child to engage in physical contact. Every parent should question whether their child has the physical ability to withstand the contact. Furthermore, hockey parents must ensure their child has the proper equipment to provide the best protection during the physical aspects of this game. Manufacturers of hockey gear have been proactive and fabricate equipment that can offset injuries to the player. The nature of the physical impact compounded by the way the child hits the boards or makes contact with the ice however, can cause serious injury.

I remember the first time my son was physically hit from behind and thrown into the boards. He was 10 years of age and the child who made the hit was of similar age. I worried that my kid's brain and body wouldn't withstand the impact. Both hockey players had been educated about the "danger zone" (ie. the area near the boards). The child who delivered the hit was obviously unable to appreciate the concept, because he had made physical contact in the danger zone. His cognitive immaturity did not permit him to fully appreciate the reasoning behind the logic of "no hitting in the danger zone". Luckily, the physical impact was limited because of the smaller body size of each child and speed of travel at the time of physical contact (Physical Impact = Velocity x Mass).

Three years later while my son was playing Minor Bantam AAA, once again he was hit from behind and thrown into the boards. The larger stature of the opponent player coupled with the velocity resulted in considerable impact into the boards. Even though my kid had an excellent protective helmet, the residual effect of the impact led to a concussion. This injury was assessed by a medical practitioner at the emergency department of a local hospital. A diagnosis of the injury showed that my kid had suffered a mild concussion. This led to the loss of two weeks of hockey activity and he had to be re-evaluated before he could return to the ice.

The Dorland's Illustrated Medical Dictionary classifies "concussion" as a violent jar or shock which causes a transient loss of consciousness with possible mild impairment of higher mental functions, or prolonged unconsciousness with impairment of the brain stem, respiratory reflex, or vasomotor activity. Kimberly Harmon in her work on the assessment and management of concussion in sport, indicates that symptoms of concussion include dizziness, headache, problems in concentration, disturbances of vision or equilibrium, loss of memory and sometimes loss of consciousness. The Hockey Trainers Certification Program indicates that the classification of concussions are commensurate with the degree and nature of the injury. Robert Cantu has addressed some of the issues regarding return to play following a concussion. His guidelines would indicate that players should return to hockey after two weeks, only if they have been asymptomatic for one week. The medical practitioner must ensure the hockey player hasn't suffered any serious brain injury. An evaluation for residual brain damage must be undertaken to ensure the hockey player can safely return to the ice.

The research of Robert Cantu, the American Academy of Neurology, the American College of Sports Medicine and the American Association of Neurological Surgeons have graded the severity of concussions into three types. "Grade I" is noted as a mild type which only involves some confusion for the player. After twenty minutes, one can return to play if he/she is asymptomatic and this is only their first concussion of the season. The second type of concussion is classified as "Grade II". This infers the child has experienced a loss of consciousness which lasts from a few seconds to an extended period. The Hockey Trainers Certification Program would indicate the child is removed from the ice on a traction board and the neck immobilized. An emergency action plan is initiated including checking the injured player's airway, breathing and circulation. An Emergency Medical Response Team is notified and the child removed from the ice by professionals who ensure the victim's airway, breathing and circulation are regularly checked. In the event the player is able to recover and get up from the ice, he/she is evaluated for nausea, headache, loss of memory, confusion, change in behaviour/ personality, lethargy, and ability to focus.

The symptoms of a Grade II injury present myriad concerns to parents, coaches and officials. These injuries have to be evaluated cautiously because of the possible long-term consequences to a player. An injured player who has experienced this type of concussion may have sustained a neck injury or brain impairment. The injured player must be quickly evaluated by a physician. The player proceeds to the hospital in the company of their parents or coach. If the player is unconscious, an ambulance transports the child to the hospital for medical evaluation. Trainers and parents are urged not to provide any pain killers until the physician has made the medical evaluation. The guidelines espoused by Robert Cantu and the American College of Sports Medicine are adamant the child should not be permitted to return to practise or play hockey until deemed ready by the physician. The amount of time could vary from week(s) to months depending on the nature, severity and the child's ability to recover from the injury.

The most serious of concussions is "Grade III". These involve unconsciousness for more than 5 minutes and loss of memory (ie. retrograde amnesia-past memories) for a period of more than 24 hours. The injured player must refrain from hockey for a period of at least one month. Following medical evaluation, the child can return to play hockey but must be cognizant that further concussions could cancel their hockey season. Recurrent traumatic brain injury is of serious consequence to the hockey player. According to David Drake and David Cifu, swelling of brain tissue and intracranial pressure can cause the brain to herniate and lead to brainstem failure causing death.

During my involvement in hockey, I have observed the impact of concussions and their residual effects on minor hockey players. In my son's case of being hit from behind, a medical evaluation showed that he experienced a Grade I concussion. He was required to refrain from playing hockey and two weeks later was re-evaluated prior to his return to the ice. Kids who experience Grade I concussions generally return to play hockey only if they don't experience repetitive concussions. Some children with second and third grade concussions leave the game of hockey for extended periods. Those who miss lengthy periods because of the serious nature of their injury have to be re-evaluated by a physician and in some cases a neurologist to ensure they are free of residual medical problems. Those kids who experience a number of second grade concussions during a hockey season are often directed to terminate their active involvement. Parents of kids who receive multiple second and third grade concussions are informed they should withdraw their child permanently from hockey. Grade II concussions could possibly lead to permanent brain injury for their child. Hockey parents should not allow their children to risk permanent brain damage by permitting them to continue a sport in which they have experienced serious medical trauma.

The brain is necessary for proper functioning of the individual. Any injury which interferes with the brain and one's cognition can have long-term debilitating effects. Every hockey player should wear proper equipment to ensure the protection of their cerebral cortex (brain). Without an intact brain, one cannot function at a high capacity in society. Brain impairment can interfere with a child's success in school and have a significant impact on one's later profession. Brent Hagel and his colleagues have noted that body-checking can cause significant injury in youngsters who are exposed to physical contact. There is documented information in medical journals to suggest that brain injuries and spine injuries have long standing negative ramifications for athletes. Any activity in which the brain is impacted by physical energy will show some temporary or permanent change. Hockey parents have to be aware that any contact sport presents a risk factor to their child. It is imperative that one use a proactive approach in any contact sport and attempt to prevent injury through education and the use of proper equipment.

It is in a parent's best interest to have their child cognitively evaluated prior to the commencement of a sport which entails physical contact. By this I am not suggesting that one obtain exhaustive medical procedures (ie. CAT, PET or MRI scans). I would advise parents however, to seek out evaluative techniques to assess their child's level of cognition. There are some psychometric tests (ie. Wechsler Intelligence; Wechsler Memory and Stanford Binet) that can act as good cognitive screening measures. These tests can be used to obtain a baseline of the child's cognitive strengths and weaknesses. The test scores can be retained for re-evaluation of cognition, if a child is physically injured and experiences first or second grade concussions. Rather than only having quantitative information (ie. number of concussions) one would also have the qualitative information (ie. nature of the injury), as a way of evaluating the degree of injury and the child's recovery of brain function. Children who experience repeated brain injury should not continue with contact sport. The hockey parent should have the necessary information to make decisions regarding their child's health. They should always weigh the risks with the benefits of a sport and should not expose their child to any form of medical danger.

I recall my concern after my child's first concussion. Having had my child tested cognitively prior to his involvement in hockey, I had a baseline in which to evaluate the impact of his brain injury. Other than the general behavioral indices (ie. his level of fatigue, sleeping pattern, ability to concentrate and grades in school), I was also privy to information which had been previously evaluated through cognitive and memory tests. This information allowed me some method of comparing his pre-hockey with post-hockey injury. A re-assessment was done approximately 6 months after the concussion for a comparative analysis. By this time his brain had some time to heal. The period between the time of injury and post-injury recovery allowed me to compare his recovery of brain function.

Neuropsychologists often refer to the brain as having some "neuroplasticity" and some "recovery of function" following injury. This infers the brain can heal and re-orient itself after accidents or injury. In other words, the brain has a certain amount of resilience that allows it to "re-boot" itself following minor damage. The localization and the extent of the injury however is of primary concern. Children vary in their ability to withstand the impact of physical brain injury. Some children recover from these incidents and others show residual side effects. The parent has to be apprised of these so they can make decisions regarding their child's cognitive health. This will allow the parent to make a decision to extract the child from hockey when there is a risk of serious harm. Parents have their motives for engaging children in the game of hockey. It is my belief that most hockey parents would quickly withdraw their child from a sport if their child was at risk for permanent brain injury.

Physical contact in hockey can lead to injury. Children are applauded by spectators when they pick themselves off the ice following physical contact by an opponent. The child will

receive treatment for their injury and most players who are injured return to the ice. In some instances where first or second
grade concussions render the child incapacitated, the return
date is delayed and this is dependent on the severity of the
injury. Players who receive injuries have to cope with the residual effects. Children who are injured in hockey must bear
the consequences of the physical injury. Some children do not
respond well to injury and experience psychological trauma
after an incident. Psychologists are sometimes consulted during the child's recovery process, especially when there are
post-traumatic consequences. Having experienced injury, the
child sometimes develops a negative conditioned response
to their injury. (eg. I was injured in hockey and experienced
some pain; therefore, I should avoid any contact in hockey that
could lead to further injury). This type of introspection by
the child, could cause an emotional reaction of anxiety/fear.
The child's anxiety or fear will surface from time to time and
prevent them from making the necessary checks on their opponents and in some cases prevent them from going into cor-
ners or against boards where contact could occur. Unless the
child is able to cope with these "negative conditioned associations" the prevailing fear will have an impact on the child's
game. Physical contact although seen as necessary in hockey,
can have long ranging psychological effects on those who have
been injured.

CONTROL OF EMOTIONS VIA ANGER MANAGEMENT PROGRAMS:

My clinical work in psychology brings me into contact with
a variety of clients who require "emotion control programs"
(ie. anger management). I have administered the Anger
Management Program to many individuals over the past 20

years. My clients come from all walks of life and have been referred because of their difficulty in managing emotions. Those
who have been referred by the court were asked to undertake
anger management because of their inability to control aggressive or assaultive behaviour. Emotion control programs assist
people in learning techniques to control their anger. Their display of aggression has often occurred in public areas and in
private domains. Clients are initially sceptical about undertaking these programs, but after completion of the Stress/Anger
Management Program, indicate the educational component has
assisted them in a better understanding and ways of controlling their aggressive behaviour.

Individuals who undertake a Stress/Anger Management
Program realize this program teaches them to recognize their
underlying emotions and to identify stressors which cause
them to respond in an angry manner. By obtaining some insight to one's emotions, allows a person to identify their internal feelings of anger. Individuals must attempt to understand
the factors which make them angry and the reasons for loss of
control. By understanding the internal mechanisms that lead
to anger, can assist one in developing coping strategies and can
prevent the expression of negative emotions (ie. aggression) by
employing strategies during times of duress.

There are many stressful situations which occur on a daily
basis. Some of these can evoke an anger response. The emotion
of anger is an acceptable behaviour as long as it doesn't occur
too often. However, when one externalizes this into aggressive
energy it can lead to hostile behaviour. A good example of anger management can be observed in the following scenario:

I had gone to a bank and was waiting for the next available
teller to serve me. When it was my turn, I approached the
desk only to be informed by the teller that she was leaving
for lunch. Undoubtedly, I was a little annoyed because there

hadn't been any indication that she was taking a break. Rather than reacting in an aggressive manner, I realized that people have work schedules to which they must adhere. When I returned to the line, I was informed by a person behind me that I should not stand in front of her because she was next in line for service. Talk about a bad day! I calmly informed the lady in an assertive manner that I had already been ahead of her and had been asked by the teller to return to the line because she was going for lunch. I informed this lady that she could pursue her business with any teller that became available to the right of us and I would pursue my business with a teller that became available to the left. A teller on the right became free and the woman promptly moved forward to take care of her business. An elderly gentleman standing behind us, had overheard the conversation and remarked "I would have told her where to go". I informed him there are three ways of acting in emotionally charged situations:

1) Aggressive Approach—telling someone off or hitting them.
2) Assertive Approach—informing them of rights and obligations and evaluating options which assist in solving a dilemma.
3) Passive Approach—allowing others to take advantage or violate one's rights by "walking over you".

I informed the elderly man that I believed in using an "assertive approach" because it diffuses an emotionally upset person and lessens the chance for verbal and physical altercation and in some cases the possibility of homicide. He agreed with me that a calm discussion is better than being killed.

A brief overview of a Stress/Anger Management Program is included in Appendix 3 for your perusal. It is based on the work of Raymond Novaco and a Video tape of this program can be obtained from IBIS Media. I trust that you will find this program of use and you will have the chance of using it in the community or at your next hockey game. We live in an emotionally charged environment with stressful routines and excessive demands. If one is equipped with a Stress and Anger Management Program, this could assist in coping with everyday stressors. It could allow for a more reasonable reaction when no other solution seems plausible.

CHAPTER SEVEN

COST OF HOCKEY

Staying physically fit is an expensive endeavour. Some sports are more costly than others and those which include the rental of facilities will create more of an expenditure for the participant. If one were content to skate on an outdoor pond or rink, the only cost would include the time taken to clear the ice surface. In society today, it isn't easy accessing an outdoor skating surface because of environmental limitations including weather, location and availability. Instead, many are faced with sporting events which require financial output. Most parents will agree that minor hockey is an expensive sport. The cost depends on the level of hockey that one plays. If a minor hockey player is happy at the house league level then the cost will be lower. If your child is not content with House League Hockey but instead wants to play at the AAA level then the cost will increase considerably. The price of hockey varies between hockey associations and is dependent on the hourly price for ice and whether the coach receives a salary. Some coaches like to practise a minimum of twice a week and this increases the fee the parent has to pay for the child's enrollment in hockey.

Minor hockey is an expensive sport but it has many advantages which outweigh its price. The cost is often similar to other high end activities including figure skating, elite dancing and gymnastics. Much of the expenses will be borne by the parent and some will come from fundraisers including sponsorships, tag days, 50/50 ticket draws, and socials (ie. comedy nights, bingos, billiard tournaments, dances). The list of social events to assist in fundraising are numerous and will be essential to defray the cost to the parent.

The best scenario that the parent can hope for is a major sponsor for your child. It would be in the parent's best interest to develop community relations with a local business sponsor and foster this relationship. Wearing the business name or logo on your child's hockey sweater will defray some of the costs for the sport. One could develop a good working relationship with the sponsor by getting friends and associates to purchase products or services from these sponsors. A good accountant will provide the ways of defraying costs by writing off many of the fees charged against the business for sponsoring community events.

The costs for organized sporting activities will include the registration fees plus the cost of equipment for the player. The total price, which includes equipment and enrollment fees, can range from $ 800 to $ 10,000 on a yearly basis depending upon the level of competition (ie. House League to AAA Midget Hockey). The aforementioned fee may not include the travelling expenses for out of town tournaments nor the cost of gasoline to transport the minor hockey player to weekly games and practises. The specific needs (ie. hockey equipment) of your child in any given year will enter the equation for the cost factor. Most children commence hockey as tyke development players. They will be involved in hockey for approximately ten years. Therefore the total cost to the parent could range from $ 8000 to $ 100,000 dollars over this 10 year period. The fee at the upper end would be decided by the child's hockey talent, league, and whether the coach is a volunteer or a salaried person. The child's interest, skills and parent's willingness to pay the expense, will be deciding factors in the hockey equation.

If the child does not have the skills or interest then the parent should not consider competitive AAA hockey because the price outlay would be of no particular advantage to the child.

Sometimes parents register their children in AA and AAA hockey leagues when the child does not have the talent nor interest in playing at this level. The outcome from these experiences can be dismal for the child who is not competent to play at this level of expertise. Placing excessive pressure on the child to excel in high level hockey when they do not have the skills, creates stress for the child. Furthermore this experience can be embarrassing for the parent, as they watch their child struggle with the plays because of their lack of skill mastery. These situations can be very taxing for a child who attempts a sport when he or she doesn't have the skills or the interest. The experience generally culminates in frustration, anger and depression for the child. Parents need to be practical in their evaluation of their child's skills and must make responsible choices. A parent should not live their lives vicariously through their children's endeavour. When a parent has failed to achieve their personal "hockey objectives" they should not attempt to accomplish these via their children. A child's interest in an activity/sport is not always consistent with the parent's choice of a sport. When the child informs the parent he/she is not interested in pursuing hockey, the parent shouldn't continue to badger the child to involve themselves in the activity. Parents must be open-minded in their perception of a child's interest and assist the child in discovering an activity which is in line with their interests. A parent should not take the stance that "my child will play hockey no matter what happens". This only serves the parent's interest and is of little value to the child who is attempting to develop their own sense of self-worth and mastery of the world.

Chapter five discussed the motivational factors that were needed by the child to excel in hockey. Every parent must consider the child's interests, skills and motivation (desire, heart) prior to involving them in minor hockey. The parent must be willing to pay the expenses and provide the transportation to the arena. Not every child, however wants to play at the competitive level. The parent must discuss their child's interest prior to registering them in this sport to ensure undue pressure is not exerted on the child.

Hockey is an expensive sport. Parents must bear in mind, that house league hockey is satisfying for most children. Parents need to evaluate their child's skills prior to enrolling him/her in hockey. With these factors considered, the parent can evaluate the child's "hockey assets" to assist them in understanding their potential for high level competition. These factors are as follows:

1) genetic ability
2) skills
3) motivation (drive/heart)
4) interest
5) physical stature

When the parent is assured the child excels at each of these five factors, the parent may decide to advance their child into the AA or AAA level of competitive hockey. The parent must assist the child in playing at a level which is commensurate with their skill level, ability and interest. Triple A hockey is for the advanced hockey player with above average skills and a competitive drive. Not every child has this ability to play hockey at a competitive level. Many hockey parents are not willing to make a personal commitment to their child by providing the time, money, and energy needed in this highly demanding sport.

Hockey parents have to do a lot of introspection and decide on what they are willing to contribute so the child can be successful in this sport. As a parent you must ask yourself what you can afford to spend on your child's hockey career and work within your budget. A child should be involved in this decision-making so they can appreciate the process. A child has to realize that hockey is an expensive sport. Parents realize that money is not always available and any high level competitive sport will strain a family's financial budget. Many parents never played high level competitive hockey because their parents couldn't afford the sport. Furthermore, most parents did not have expensive equipment but used second had equipment in their pursuit of this game. In modern society, kids are better equipped to play hockey because their parents have more disposable income.

The Equipment:

I am not going to spend much time extolling the virtues of equipment. The two most important pieces of equipment the parent has to consider are the helmet and the skates. The helmet must by of top quality and have safety features to protect the child's brain. In an earlier chapter, I expanded on the concept of injury. I attempted to make the reader aware of the seriousness of brain injuries (ie. concussions) and the impact on the child's health. When children experience brain injury, this can adversely impact on health and can negatively effect scholastic performance and later professional goals. Furthermore, damage to the brain can have some long lasting effects on the child's capacity to function normally.

HELMET.

The helmet must be of high quality and have the necessary protection to ensure safety to the child. The cerebral cortex is not fully developed in the youngster. The brain will not reach maturity until 20-25 years. Any physical damage to the brain can have long ranging effects on one's cognitive ability. A child's head can be easily injured in any contact sport. Major concussions (Grade II or III) can cause minor and/or major brain impairment. These will often times end one's career in hockey and could cause life-long debilitating effects. Parents must be vigilant of their child's health and purchase the best helmet on the market. In 2007, it cost between $150.00 to $300.00 dollars for a well constructed helmet that could provide adequate protection to one's brain. This expenditure will offer the parent some peace of mind knowing they have used a proactive approach to their child's safety and well-being. A parent does not benefit from purchasing a "pre-owned hockey helmet", because this piece of equipment may have been previously damaged when its owner made contact with the boards or the ice. The integrity of the helmet's structure could limit the protective value for the child.

SKATES:
The next important piece of equipment to consider would have to be the skates. I have discussed the advantages of protection offered by a well constructed helmet. Equally important are the skates which must have the physical integrity to support the ankles and arch. Skates must consist of the right design so the child can learn to skate efficiently. Without the proper skates, the child will never learn the skating skills which are necessary for agility and speed. In today's market, "pre-owned skates" are available to the consumer. Some parents cannot afford the cost of new skates and are often only prepared to spend fewer dollars because children out-grow skates quickly. The problem with "pre-owned skates" is that they have often taken on the shape of the last person's foot. This could become a problem for the skater who must accommodate the "foot

shape" of the previous owner and will impede their skating ability. Pre-owned skates may be alright for the recreational skater who is occasionally involved in this activity but may not serve the best interests of the athlete who needs proper fitting, protective skates to enhance their on-ice skills. A young hockey player has to repeatedly engage in drills during practise sessions and ill-fitting skates will not provide the needed support. A parent should attempt to purchase skates that will mould to the child's feet. Proper fitting skates ensure the right gait for the child, which invariably translates into balance and agility on ice.

There are other important pieces of equipment in hockey but I will not extol on their virtues. The parent who is interested in ice hockey can speak directly to proprietors of sports stores. Parents should ensure that prior to purchasing equipment for their child, they interact with people who have expert knowledge of hockey equipment. Part-time salespeople can sometimes provide erroneous information because they are employed on a hourly rate to sell a product. Although these individuals have good intentions, they do not always have the knowledge to provide detailed information about the hockey product.

In summary, there are many costs to hockey. The physical, mental and emotional cost of this game will far outweigh the monetary costs. Parents have to be proactive in any undertaking to ensure they obtain the best product for their money. Any recreational activity that one pursues, whether it be bowling or hockey, has a dollar value that must be considered prior to becoming involved in the sport. I know of some parents who would not invest a dime in their children's sporting activities. These people come from all walks of life and some have the financial means to provide a recreational outlet for their children. Their unwillingness to provide the funds so their children can enjoy recreation could merely be a reflection of their miserliness. It is prudent for parents to involve their children in sport because of its many benefits, including physical conditioning and cardiovascular health. As I noted earlier, obesity rates for children are approximately 30% for children in Canada. Recently the Canadian government offered some incentive to improving physical health by allowing parents to deduct $500 dollars yearly on their taxes for each child involved in some athletic activity. It is wise to invest in a child's extracurricular activities so they will develop healthy bodies. This will far outweigh the medical expenses associated with illness and physical maladies created by inactive and unhealthy people.

CHAPTER EIGHT

SUCCESS IN HOCKEY: THE STATISTICS

E very child has a chance of success in hockey. Some are genetically endowed and display talent in their skills and presence on the ice. Other players are bound by drive and heart for the game. There are players who have a combination of talent and skills, which help them achieve their goals. Many children have attributes which allow them to advance to the next level of hockey. These factors will determine the child's objectives and their success in the game of hockey.

During adolescence, a hockey player undergoes many cognitive changes. Advancement in cognition during this stage of development is of paramount importance to the adolescent's growth. The adolescent involved in hockey begins to look at new ways of adjusting their skills to the game. This can be advantageous to one's advancement in minor hockey. At other times, it can prove to be a disadvantage because with the physical growth spurt that accompanies pubescence, some adolescents become awkward and uncoordinated in their sensory and motor processing. This can create agility problems for some players as they attempt to adjust to new physiological demands. Although adolescents' analytical skills improve as they enter the formal stage (13 to 19 years) of cognitive development, they may be disadvantaged in the synchronization of performance skills because of the physical awkwardness which begins with this stage.

Hockey parents must be realistic in their appraisal of a kid's hockey talent. Good talent at the Double A or Triple A level of hockey does not infer that a child is going to make it to the Provincial, State, American or National Hockey Leagues. The skills a child possesses during their formative years are not always carried forward to adolescence. There are many hockey players who were talented as youngsters but lose their interest in hockey as they age. A multitude of problems including parental pressure, poor coaching, lack of motivation, confidence, employment or other pursuits, often impede a player's advancement in this sport.

The hockey parent must maintain an open mind about their child's success in hockey. The fable of "sour grapes" too often enters the picture especially when the parent fails to evaluate the child's talents realistically. Rationalization is a great defense mechanism when the child fails to make a team. The parent often cries "foul" when the adolescent is not favoured because of the "politics of hockey". Sometimes the parent will point a finger at a coach or organization for their mismanagement of a young hockey player. In the final analysis, the child and the parent must bear the consequence of the outcome. Every kid cannot make it to the next level of hockey. There are many kids playing in the minor hockey league and very few places to go in higher level hockey. Most minor hockey teams are only equipped to select 15 players and 2 goalies. The parent has to face the facts that there just aren't enough teams to accommodate every kid. If more kids were selected on minor hockey teams, players would see very little ice time and this would create greater frustration and more problems.

Life is not always fair and neither is hockey. The coaches generally do their best to get the most out of every kid. Scouts carefully evaluate kids at provincial tournaments and do their best to select those kids with hockey talent. Many people collectively do their best to evaluate great players but every kid does not have the potential of making the big league. Some coaching staff do make mistakes in their selection process and talented kids may be overlooked. Decisions aren't always favourable and at other times the selection of hockey players doesn't work out. When a child isn't selected to a team, there is very little the parent can do about it.

Life is not a bowl of cherries and what you expect from hockey and what happens in this sport is often beyond one's control. When your kid doesn't make the team, attempt to assist them in resolving the issue of rejection. Rather than blaming coaches or scouts for their incompetence, the parent has to assist the youngster in resolving their dilemma of "tryout rejection". The re-building of self-esteem has to be implemented so the child can regain their self-confidence. Don't allow your kid to wallow in self-pity. Misery likes miserable company and commiserating about not being selected on a hockey team only makes the child feel worse. Low self-esteem may lead to depressive feelings and depression only lowers the mood of the child. Sigmund Freud noted that depressed people are symptomatic of those who have turned their anger on themselves. People who blame themselves for personal shortcomings can become despondent and sometimes suicidal. Rather than blaming oneself for not being selected to a team, it is better for the child to harness the anger. In this way this kinetic energy can be re-channelled into positive growth and used to assist the child in training harder to make the next team.

By the time an adolescent is 15 years of age, they have reached the status of Midget level hockey. Highly skilled players with talent will move forward to the Triple A Midget level and those who are less talented will play Triple A Minor Midget, Double A or House League Midget hockey. An adolescent must have hockey talent, good skating ability, reasonable physical stature and hockey smarts to advance to the Triple A Midget league. Hockey players come in different shapes and sizes. Their success in hockey is determined by their ability to play with other advanced athletes. There are some talented players who will naturally move to Junior A, Provincial or State leagues. Many others will compete in Triple A, College or University hockey leagues. The sky is the limit for talented hockey players. There will always be a scout at a tournament intent on finding a star who will rise to the highest level of hockey.

Many hockey parents are an anxious and competitive group. They want to know which players will make it. My opinion is that every kid who has played hockey and has had some fun in the game has made it in hockey. The hockey parent who is concerned with their child "making it to the big league" has to keep a number of factors in mind. Research by Jim Parcels in 1995 entitled "the chances of making it in pro hockey" provides some insight to this question. Parcels did some longitudinal research in which he investigated the outcome for approximately 30,000 players involved in minor hockey in Ontario. He evaluated the data on boys who had been born in 1975. In 1991 these boys were in their 16th birthday year and eligible for the Ontario Hockey League draft. According to Jim Parcels, 232 boys of the 30,000 players who had been registered in Ontario Minor Hockey were selected for the draft that year. Parcels' statistics further showed that of the 232 Ontario players, approximately 105 (45%) played at least one game in the OHL. Of these 105 players, only 90 (38%) completed their eligibility of 3 to 4 years in the OHL, and only 42 (18%) played in the NCAA hockey division. Furthermore, of the 30,000 hockey players, only 48 (0.16%; 16 in every 10,000) were drafted by NHL teams. Of these 48 players, only 32 (0.11%; 11 in every 10,000) competed in one NHL game; and of the 32 players only 15 (0.05%; 5 in every 10,000) played more than one full NHL season. Last, only 6 (0.02%; 2 in every 10,000) would complete a minimum of 400 games, the approximate number of games played over a five year period.

It should become clear to parents that the odds of any kid making it to the big league is indeed slim. Only 6 players out of the 30,000 Ontario player pool born in 1975 played at least one full season in the NHL. This infers that only 1 of every 5,000 young hockey players made it to the big league for a minimum 5 year period. The hockey parent will surmise from these statistics that very few kids will make it to the NHL. To make it to the big league, a child needs a number of factors in their favour. These include genetic hockey ability, which influences a player's hockey skills at passing, shooting and scoring; and physical size, because larger statured players don't get pushed around as much as smaller players. This latter factor is especially important for defencemen who must have the ability to control action around the net. There are always exceptions to the rule and there are some cases of small players making it, but these players usually occupy forward positions. Motivation is another important variable in the selection process. Motivation is also known as drive, interest or heart for the game. Players must he willing to give 100% to every game they play. Coaches who don't see this enthusiasm are not likely to give the hockey player much time on the ice. In Triple A leagues where winning is an important aspect of the game, the coach is vigilant of players who give the game everything they've got. Players who are slow, don't make good passes or can't score are not given good ratings by coaches or scouts. The adolescent Triple A player is usually playing at a high level because they are interested in furthering their hockey career. The player who does not produce on ice is not likely to advance to the ncxt level (ie. OHL, Junior A or NCAA). There is little room for the player who does not play the game at a high level. These players are not selected to a higher level of hockey and generally will find their hockey careers over in mid-adolescence.

The statistics are clear from Jim Parcels research. Only one out of every five thousand kids will make it to the NHL and stay for a minimum of five years. Connections in sport are important but one still needs the skills and the determination to get there. One of the last things needed is luck. Timing is everything and being in the right place at the right time is often beneficial. For example, if a player gets injured and another player gets the chance to show their "stuff on ice", this could lead to a favourable outcome. Another situation is one where a kid is at a tournament and gets noticed by a scout. A hockey player needs a lucky break in this sport. Some talented hockey players make it to the big league but have a bad season. They fail to impress the coach and find themselves back in the minors. This generally leads to the player's demise in big league hockey. When a player makes it to the NHL level and then is sent back to the minors, there is a very slim chance of making a return to the NHL.

The Ontario statistics compiled by Jim Parcels are only a small part of the picture. Minor hockey players must remember that in Canada there are 10 Provinces and 3 Territories. One must add the 50 States in the USA, the European Countries and for that matter the rest of the planet. A perusal of statistics compiled by Dan Diamond and colleagues in their book entitled "Total Hockey" would indicate that some players are born in other countries including South America and India. In their 2003 edition, Diamond and his associates provide copious data for the consumer of hockey fact. These researchers noted that between 1917 and 2003 approximately 5,610 forwards, defencemen and goalies saw action in the NHL. Close inspection of the individual player statistics indicate that approximately 45 percent of these hockey stars lasted for a minimum of 5 years or more in the NHL. This would imply that making it to NHL hockey does not provide any assurance to the hockey player they will stay within the ranks of the hockey heroes. Unless players produce on the ice, they will be shipped back to the affiliated leagues. The majority (approximately 55 %) of the 5,610 hockey players who made it to NHL between 1917 to 2003 lasted fewer than five seasons and many lost status with the NHL league after only one season. One has to wonder whether scouts in their over zealousness had selected players who really shouldn't have made it in the first place, or whether the players selected just weren't that talented when they had to produce on ice at the NHL level. There must be reasons for the demise of almost 55 % of the players who couldn't remain beyond the 5 year period.

Parents need to realize that many kids dream of making it big in the NHL. The bottom line, is that few kids will make it to this level of hockey. It isn't of any benefit to put pressure on kids to excel with the expectation they will make it to the big league. Hockey parents should always keep the dream alive for every youngster. Parents must remember that the chances of making it to the NHL hockey are better than the odds of winning a lottery in Canada. Kids deserve to have the chance to play hockey. However, they don't need constant pressure on them to excel. I often tell parents they should never get their hopes up that their kid will make it to the NHL. It is nice to dream and dreams are what we often live for and every person needs a dream. Humans strive to attain the things they don't have. Dreaming is beneficial to the human psyche and it assists one in coping with the mundane aspects of everyday life. People dream of winning lotteries but in reality, the chance of winning the "big one" is about 1 out of 14,000,000 (0.000007

%). However, it seems that someone always wins the lottery and it is just a matter of timing and luck.

Rather than worrying about a kid's future in the NHL, one should count the benefits of minor hockey. Parents get enjoyment from watching their kids play this game. Hockey is entertaining and provides relief from daily life stressors. Hockey parents have to be cognizant that adolescents who play hockey are constantly under pressure to excel. They worry their coaches and the scouts who evaluate them, won't recognize their talent. These young hockey hopefuls express anxiety regarding their ability to make it to the next level of competitive hockey. They will undergo much misery as they aspire to get drafted to higher level hockey, especially if the parent places pressure on them. The point here is that very few kids will make it to the Provincial level. Those who do make it, won't get much ice-time unless they are highly talented hockey players. Many "ride the pine" and warm the bench for the senior more experienced members of the team. You have been provided with the statistics by Jim Parcels and Dan Diamond and his colleagues. The hockey parent must realize that by creating the expectation that your kid will make it to NHL is placing much undue pressure on them. If your reason for enrolling your kid in hockey was because of the belief your child would make it to the NHL, then you should re-evaluate your goals and your strategies for your kid's success.

Hockey parents must be reasonable and come to the understanding that very few kids will make it to the NHL. The best thing that a hockey parent can do is enjoy every practise and every game. Minor hockey is about fun, friendships, exercise and relationships with others. These are the important benefits of playing the game and become the most important facet of hockey. This sport teaches kids cooperation with others, respect for others and most importantly, respect for oneself. By taking the time to learn this sport, the child can obtain much satisfaction as they learn new skills. Hockey is a simple game which requires myriad skills, analytical thinking and quick decision-making. Hockey is a game that can provide joy from winning and sadness from defeat. Minor hockey will inspire and motivate many players to learn an activity that can be carried throughout one's life. A person will never forget how to skate once they have learned this skill. Any senior hockey player will tell you they play the game for fun. In their mind they can relive every great hockey experience they've come to know in hockey. They can attempt these plays in their on-ice games. Minor hockey is not about fame or fortune. This game is about the memories that are created on ice and carried into later life.

CHAPTER NINE

THE EPILOGUE: MINOR HOCKEY AND THE LONG ROAD TO NHL

Every hockey player has a story to tell about their initiation into the world of minor hockey. Like the majority of others who played hockey, some achieved the highest status their natural talent, skills, motivation, and connections would allow. The sport of hockey taught players about their inner dynamics and instilled the rules and the principles of diligence on the ice. Minor hockey players learned cooperation, teamanship and had some fun while they played this game.

Some children undertake the activity of hockey because they like the sport. Others will tell you they played hockey during their childhood but as they became adolescents they pursued other sports, part-time employment or personal relationships. Some pursued hockey because they had a dream of making it the NHL, whereas others pursued this sport because it provided exercise and friendships. Others have continued playing this sport well into their senior years. For many in the old-timer leagues, the game of hockey never ends but just gets put over until the following week.

When hockey was first created, it was not intended to be a full-time career for those who played the game. Athletes who originally played NHL hockey were not paid for their participation. These players worked in menial jobs to supplement their meagre NHL wages. Professional sports have their benefits but hockey has only recently come of age. It was only in the last 30 years that hockey players started receiving substantial monetary benefits for their involvement in this game. Players are now being paid in accordance with their output on ice.

Hockey is a physically demanding sport. The athlete in this sport must be in excellent physical condition to endure constant body-contact during the game. Most hockey players only last 12 to 15 years before they are forced or decide to retire. Those who play professional NHL hockey today, will agree that hockey is financially rewarding but love of the game drives the players. This sport dictates that players live out of a suitcase for 8 to 10 months of the year for the duration of their hockey career. Interviews with professional hockey players leave one to conclude that physical injuries, travel and absence from one's family create some duress. The money an NHL player earns properly compensates them for their commitment to this sport but does not compensate the player for their loss of time with family and friends.

Over the last decade, I have talked to many children in the hockey arena. Very few have told me they wanted to make it to the NHL because of the money they would receive in this sport. The parents of these minor hockey players may have had some notion of financial gain, but most kids state they play hockey because they like the sport. During my formative years in Northern Ontario, hockey was an activity that one played because the outside conditions allowed it to happen. It took place on the road, pond, or outdoor rink. It happened because children wanted to get out of the house and engage in a recreational activity that was fun and reduced the boredom of winter.

In the 1950's, there wasn't any concern about obesity in children. In that era, children enjoyed physical activity and were challenged by their environment. When children weren't in the classroom, they were engaged in hobbies or involved in sports. Parents did not have to persuade their children to get off the couch or put down the computer games or videos. Our entertainment existed through physical activities that evolved with the seasonal changes. Baseball happened in the spring, swimming in the summer, football in the fall, skating and hockey in the winter.

In Northern Ontario, one needed a hobby because winters were long. Playing hockey was a good way to spend one's time because this activity was relatively inexpensive and only required a stick and a pair of skates. I grew up in a small town and first learned to skate on a frozen pond. Winter in my northern community was cold and its first sign was measured by the ice on the frozen ponds. While walking to school each day, the thickness of the ice was tested by tossing rocks on the frozen ponds. Kids could predict with some degree of accuracy when the ice would be ready for hockey. With the oncoming cold winter days, the ice would freeze and hockey would begin. It was at this time that we could become hockey players and identify with our favourite NHL teams. A kid could become an imaginary hockey star and grace the frozen ponds with their skills.

It didn't matter which of the original six hockey teams one was assigned, as long as one could engage in this sport. With time, every kid could choose the team of their dreams. Every kid could become a hockey star but not any kid could be Gordie Howe, Bobby Hull, Maurice Richard, Frank Mahovlich, or Jonnie Bower. One had to earn this status by the skills displayed during competition. The right to become an NHL star had to be gained by one's playing ability. With time all kids became legendary heroes in their own minds but would return to their own identities after the game was over. Motivation to play hockey was determined by one's output on the ice. Each

child measured his success by the way he played on a particular day and every day thereafter until winter had run its
course. With time, winter would make its transition to spring
and the outdoor rinks would melt. Skates and hockey sticks
would be relegated to a corner of a basement or shed.

Hockey was never an organized sport in the small town
in which I was raised. It was merely an activity that occurred
because the winter season permitted it to happen. I was born
in the era when only six hockey teams existed (ie. Toronto
Maple Leafs, Montreal Canadians, Detroit Red Wings, New
York Rangers, Boston Bruins, and the Chicago Black Hawks).
I remember those Saturday evenings sitting in front of our
black and white Philco television as the rivals battled it out on
the ice. My two favourite teams were Toronto and Montreal.
Call it old time patriotism, but a young Canadian couldn't sell
out to the teams south of the border just because they had
great stars like Gordie Howe or Bobby Hull. Kids would talk
hockey at school and during winter recess the teachers would
let us practise our skills on the school rink. It was at these
times that reality could become transfixed into fantasy and
our daydreams would prevail as we took to the ice. A toss of
the coin would decide our fate and the winner would have first
choice of becoming the team of their fancy. It was at this time
that one would become the imaginary players of our dreams.
We could develop identities based on our knowledge of our
Saturday night hockey heroes.

I have always wondered what it takes to make it to big
league hockey. I have pondered that question since my early
hockey experience on the frozen ponds. I have written this
book from a hockey parent's perspective because unlike many
talented hockey players who made it to the big league, I did
not possess the skills. Genetically, I showed more promise as
an "armchair athlete". Over the years I have come to realize

that one must have a unique combination of skills to make it to the big league. Research has shown that people are unique and have specific genetic skills. The type of skills that one needs in hockey, must equip them with the "hockey smarts" needed for the professional development in this sport.

Howard Gardner has noted there are at least 7 different types of intelligence. These styles of intelligence equip people to function efficiently in some chosen field. It is possible that some individuals possess all 7 types but the probability of this occurring is generally quite slim. Every kid who plays hockey may not have the particular sensory-motor or kinesthetic-body intelligence that prepares them for the hockey arena. Consequently, if one does not have the particular type of talent that equips them for the ice, they may not be genetically endowed to excel at this chosen sport. Coaches and scouts provide the external evaluation to assist the hockey athlete in recognizing their talent. Every hockey player however, must do some self-evaluation to ensure they have the skills to advance in this sport. Talented hockey players require the sensory-motor, kinesthetic and spatial intelligence which prepare them for the game of hockey. Many players have these advanced skills because of their genetic nature. Although there isn't any quick test to evaluate this "genetic marker", in time scientists will undoubtedly develop the "litmus test" which allows one insight to recognize the chromosome and the genes responsible for this biological talent.

Children in North America who play hockey, attempt to learn the skills so they can excel in this sport. Many hockey kids want to move to the competitive level. These young hockey players are motivated by their internal drives. At times, kids are pressured by their parent's ulterior motives, even when the young player doesn't have the genetic ability. Don't get me wrong, it is important to have motivated hockey parents,

otherwise there wouldn't be anyone to drive the child to practises or games. The hockey parent must always bear in mind
however, that a child's success in this sport can come in many
different forms. Sometimes it is merely the gains achieved in
the child's hockey skills and not always determined by medals,
trophies or making it to the big league.

Many memorable times can be gained from one's experience as a hockey parent. One's skills in adapting to the role as
a hockey parent can be achieved through interaction with others. One needs a sense of humour and friendships with other
hockey parents to benefit from this sport. These attributes assist one to adapt to the demands of this sport. Parents come
to realize that minor hockey is an activity which provides fun,
skills and friendships for the child. Some of these skills are
transferable and can become generalized to social interaction
with others later in life. Listening, adhering to rules, working
hard, and respecting others are only a few of the skills that
one learns from this team sport. The hockey parent needs to
become cognizant of the dynamics of child development and
its impact on minor hockey players.

Hockey has always been Canada's winter passion. The
dream of making it to the NHL, has become a focal point for
many kids who are involved in this sport. The statistics seem
to support the notion that Canadian and American players
have become the main contenders and the "power houses" in
hockey. The point that I make here, is that North American
hockey players have excelled in their skills and sportsmanship.
When minor hockey players say they want to become NHL
stars, they should be taken seriously. Children should be encouraged to learn the skills and play to the best of their ability
so they can make it to the NHL. Every child who has uttered
an interest in big league hockey has to be taught the skills that
will make them successful athletes in this sport. Coaches can

provide the training to these determined young athletes but the ultimate motivation has to come from the player.

Any parent who has watched or played hockey knows that when one team gets a lead in hockey, a challenge is created. The psychology of sports seems to prevail in these circumstances and the team with motivation, skills and endurance appears to rise to become the victorious competitor. Children need to be encouraged by their parents and coaches to cope with the emotional demands of hockey. Children have to develop their psyche (mind) and learn to use mental imagery so they have the advantage in competitive games. Hockey parents need to be supportive of their children so the emotional burden experienced in games does not crush the child's urge to play at their highest level.

Hockey is a unique sport. Unlike many other sports it takes a combination of skills to become a good player. First and foremost, one must know how to skate and perform this task with finesse. This not only requires forward mobility but also ability to skate backwards and laterally. Added to this, is the ability to stick handle and while in motion, pass the puck accurately to a team mate. These skills become the important motor abilities that are found in the game of hockey. In terms of rank order the second most important factor is the hockey player's level of motivation ("the heart") to work diligently at every practice and every game. One is required to have that added drive and demonstrate one's best effort every second of the game. Many kids have the genetic ability, skills and the motivation for hockey but only a few will make it to the NHL.

Hockey kids come in different shapes and sizes. It appears that size may not be the most important asset when evaluating overall ability because there are some smaller statured hockey players who have made it to the big league. There are always exceptions to every rule. Scouts and coaches will sometimes examine a combination of features that are needed to suit their team. If the hockey player is extremely talented but smaller in size, a position on the forward line would be commensurate with their ability. Smaller statured players with good skills, physical stamina and endurance can make the grade. Hockey players assigned to a defensive role however have to be of larger stature. This makes sense to coaches, because the larger statured player can stop the opposing player. So the tip to the hockey parent should be clear. If your child is of smaller stature it isn't of any benefit to encourage them to undertake the task of a defensive player. Even though your child may have the skills, physical prowess and endurance, he may not be of large enough stature to stop the opponent. When it comes to defencemen "bigger is better". Size is important because this allows the defenceman greater reach in blocking or stopping shots.

For the past ten years I have observed young players in organized hockey. Chronological age is an important factor when considering the achievement potential of the budding hockey player. The sooner your child learns to skate, the sooner they can practise their hockey skills. The best teacher of these skills are the organizations that offer "skating programs". These organizations impart skating skills through their conditioning programs. The child enroled in these programs will learn balance, coordination, forward and backward propulsion techniques.

A child's skills will determine their potential and level of achievement in minor hockey. No level of pressure exerted by scouts, coaches, hockey organizations, or hockey parents can dictate a child's personal success or potential for success. Generally kids commence hockey at age 5. As they progress in this sport, many embrace the dream of becoming big league hockey stars. The reality however, is that most hockey players will not achieve this status. Hockey parents, must realize that in order to achieve the ultimate dream of the NHL, the young budding hockey player requires skills, motivation, physical strength, endurance and the hockey connections, if they are to be noticed by coaches or scouts. Hockey parents must remember that they cannot cajole, bully or buy their kids a spot in the big league.

Hockey skills can not be achieved through the educational system but only achieved through genetics, motivation and practise. Many kids have the basic skills needed to play minor hockey. They are motivated to work diligently at this sport and have the physical ability required to play in high level games. Many hockey players are insightful and can move the puck up the ice and put it in the net. These talents seem to be a natural genetic gift. It creates a player with the unique sensory-motor ability which allows them to coordinate hand and eye ability with their skating skills. These skills allow the young hockey player to move the puck to his or her team mates and to score on the goalie. Ostensibly, a combination of skills are needed to perform this feat. These include genetic talent, training and internalized motivators that allow the young hockey player to achieve the highest level of skill development.

Being a good hockey parent also requires a number of skills. I have expanded on these throughout this book because it is imperative these skills are utilized adequately to assist your kid. The techniques that I have included in earlier chapters will provide you with the parenting advice to encourage your child during their hockey game. Hockey parents must shell out the cash for registration, equipment, skill development and transportation to the practices and games. The parent can only do so much to enhance the child's chance of making it to the NHL. With the right psychological tools, the parent however, can at least motivate the child to the highest level of hockey development. Encouragement and praise go a long way to augment your child's skills. Ridicule, antagonism and pressure will only disable the child before he or she gets started. Positive input by the parent can assist the child in acquiring their dream. A hockey parent must remember that their aspiration for the big league doesn't mean the child will make it. The statistics are clear and although 90 percent of the kids want to make it to the NHL, only 0.02 percent (1 out of 5000 players) will achieve long term status in the big league.

The hockey parent must remember that minor hockey is not about making it to the NHL. The most important aspect of a child's journey through life is learning personal skills that will make them adaptive as adults. The positive experiences the child acquires in childhood and adolescence will take them to their next level of development. Parents need to exude a positive attitude toward minor hockey players. Many kids have succumbed to the negative demands of parents who have placed too much emphasis on winning. The following statements are important reminders that critical comments and pressure never provide the minor hockey player with anything but negativism and a negative attitude ruins a child's self-worth:

1) **"That's the worst game you ever played"**
2) **"You'll never make it to the NHL playing that way"**
3) **"There are scouts in the crowd watching you"**

Children respond positively to praise and react badly to criticism. Self-worth is enhanced by encouragement not by negativity. Thinking back to the most successful hockey players that I have known, I realize these players had particular skills that propelled them to the big league. To play well in the game of hockey, a kid needs the right genetic material, physical stature, motivation and proper coaching. To be an effective hockey player, one also has to have a desire to play the game of hockey. But most important in this formula of success is that parents provide the emotional support to their children:

1) PARENTS MUST USE POSITIVE REINFORCEMENT TO SHAPE THEIR CHILDREN'S EXPERIENCES.

2) HOCKEY PARENTS MUST PROVIDE THE ENCOURAGEMENT AND INITIATIVE TO ENSURE THEIR CHILD MAKES EVERY PRACTICE AND GAME.

3) HOCKEY PARENTS SHOULD PROVIDE UNCONDITIONAL POSITIVE REGARD, SO THEIR CHILDREN FEEL GOOD ABOUT THEMSELVES EVERY MINUTE OF THE GAME.

4) A GOOD HOCKEY PARENT WILL ALWAYS BE AVAILABLE TO GO THE EXTRA MILE.

With solid output in the game, the hockey parent should provide positive encouragement to the child. If the game does not favour the child, the hockey parent should never express dismay, negativism or disdain. Comments should never be made to negate the child's actions during the game. There is one important rule of thumb that the parent can learn about the game of hockey; "it is better to say nothing to the child who has not performed well in the game than to ridicule or belittle them".

Life is full of positive experiences which a hockey parent can savour. The aroma of coffee in the morning, signifies the wake-up call for the early morning practise. In minor hockey there will be many cups of coffee to awaken the parent. If you don't like getting up early, then you had better not enrol your child in minor hockey. For some reason, young hockey players always get the earliest and the worst practise times. Perhaps this is done intentionally by hockey organizations to ensure the parent becomes fully aware of the commitment needed to get their children to the arena. It almost seems as though the early morning practises are initiated as some "right of passage into the world of minor hockey". The hockey parent and the young players are forced to pay their dues for undertaking this experience. Practise times don't get any better until your child is older. The parent has to learn to tolerate early morning practises or think about enrolling their child in another sport. Some of my friends have their children enrolled in swimming. They tell me that practises for young swimmers begin as early as 5:00 a.m. At least by 6:00 a.m. most parents have rested sufficiently to get their child to the arena on time.

One of the things that hockey parents learn early in life is that ice-time is difficult to get. There is much competition these days to get prime ice times. Many minor hockey teams compete for the prime times and getting accustomed to the early morning rise, seems to be consistent with the dictates of minor hockey. Sometimes one will encounter hockey parents who attempt to shirk their responsibilities by not getting to the early morning practises. Some parents also attempt to pass this responsibility onto the coach or other parents. If your kid wants the chance of making it to the big league, a parent should not pass on their responsibility to others. There are no guaranties in hockey and no guaranties in life. Not every kid is going to make it to the NHL. But with the parent's input and assistance, every kid has the chance of making it.

Hockey parents have observed the smile on their kid's face after winning a game or scoring a goal. Hockey parents must remember that their commitment will ensure that their child learns the skills and discipline in this sport. The parent will develop a sense of pride and satisfaction as they come to realize they are assisting their youngsters in accomplishing the skills needed to propel their talent. Some children quickly adapt to skating and others will struggle. Kids are not created with similar talent but can learn to skate well with perseverance and positive motivation from the parent. Providing the encouragement by uttering "way to go, good skating, nice attempt" is positive and this type of reinforcement serves to shape a child in their pursuit. Your child is going to have to learn to skate before he or she can play the game of hockey.

A parent can't predict the future for their kid in any sport. A good hockey parent can only assist the child and encourage performance in the sport. Being a good hockey parent will allow you to assist with your child's development. By showing non-critical judgement will ensure that your child advances in this sport. Remember the words of encouragement are more important to your child than words of discouragement. By maintaining a positive attitude will ensure that your child has the chance of making it to their highest level of success.

Dreams come in different shapes and sizes. Every kid does not have the same dream, and at times the dreams the child and parent have are dissimilar. In the game of hockey, a parent can enjoy many experiences with the child. At times, the parent will wonder what possessed them to enrol their kid into a sport that forced them to sit in a cold and damp arena. But as the parent observes their child's progress and accomplishments, they experience a sense of pride in their child. In quiet contemplation, this experience allows the parent to reflect on the collective memories that one has of the child's struggle to attain their ultimate goal. As a parent, you will wonder whether it was the smile on your child's face or the small gains they made as they struggled at their sport. Regardless of what motivated your decision to assist your child with their minor hockey career, you come to realize the sport of hockey has assisted in child-parent bonding. The hockey experience has provided the opportunity for the parent to know their child. Long

after the experience of hockey has run its course, these memories will provide for many parent-child discussions. The dream
of stardom in the NHL allows the child to develop their skills.
The game of hockey brings the parent into close contact with
a child's aspirations. It permits an enriched conversation with
a youngster who has the facts about hockey stored in their
memory banks. The memories of hockey last a life time.

Goals in life are based on one's dreams. Parents are willing
to assist their children with their goals. When a child talks of
becoming an astronaut or a doctor, parents encourage these
aspirations because they want their child to accomplish goals.
Parents often remind their children that it's important to do
well in school. Listening to the teacher and doing homework
is encouraged by parents because it is their belief that these
attributes will get the child closer to their professional aspirations. Children need to be constantly reminded that they need
"back up plans" in case their primary objectives are thwarted.
Children must be encouraged to attain their schooling but at
the same time, a parent should also ensure the child has extracurricular activities. If hockey is the activity the child chooses,
the parent should be willing to assist the child in his or her
advancement in this sport.

Perusal of the hockey research will remind you of the facts.
The data collected by Jim Parcels shows that only 1 out of
5,000 players makes a life-long career for themselves in the
NHL. Furthermore, the data collected by Dan Diamond and
his colleagues indicate that approximately 45 % of those players
who make it in NHL stay at least 5 years or more. Regardless
of the statistics, every kid who begins hockey has a chance of
making it to the big league. Every parent has seen the names,
pictures and jersey numbers of the players who have made it
to the NHL, posted on the walls of their community arenas.
Many hockey parents dream of their child's name on the same

wall with the NHL hockey greats. Regardless of the chance of your child making it to the NHL, hockey parents should do their utmost to allow their youngsters to learn the skills that are needed to become hockey stars. Hockey parents are motivated to assist their children in obtaining their goals.

Hockey parents must believe in their child because every 5 year old has a chance of making it to the big league. By the time your child has attained adolescent status you will become aware of your kid's chance of success in hockey because this can be measured by the number of phone calls they receive from coaches or scouts looking for talented players. For those parents whose kid has the skills and are recognized by the agents who represent the NHL teams, a sense of accomplishment is experienced. For the countless other hockey parents whose child doesn't get the important telephone calls, all is not lost. This allows you to return to reality and recognize the goals your child has accomplished in minor hockey.

Hockey parents spend considerable money in developing their children's skills. It is easy to rationalize the cost of hockey because this is minuscule when you come to appreciate your child's accomplishments in this sport. Having encouraged your child to play this sport, you begin to understand that hockey is not only about winning or making it to the big league. Your child's involvement in hockey has taught them a number of life skills. On a more encompassing level, it has taught them respect for others and for themselves. Team membership has taught them the skills of listening to the coach, following directions, and interacting with other children. These skills will assist them as they go forward with their lives and careers. Whether or not they become great hockey players, the "team skills" have made them better community-minded and will assist them in working with others as they develop their professions.

Hockey parents also benefit greatly from their involvement in this activity. Hockey allows the parent to develop community spirit and become part of a group that advocates for the development of children. Parents come to learn that talented hockey players are equipped with internal skills that are nurtured through their learning experience. Every kid has a chance of making it big in hockey. Sometimes this accomplishment will come in small increments and will include every new skill learned in practises and measured by success in games and tournaments. A kid may never make it to the NHL but without dreams they would have little to base their existence. Life is short but it can be very meaningful, especially if one has a goal. As one engages in the drudgery of the endless tasks and routines which make life mundane and sometimes pointless, small dreams allow one to transfix themselves to a better place. Hockey parents know the chances of their child making the NHL are not in their favour. There are 30 NHL hockey teams and someone has to fill these positions, it could be your child who makes the cut.

REFERENCES

Allport, G. (1966) Traits Revisited. American Psychologist, 21, 1-10.

Anderson, S.J. (2000) Safety in Youth Ice Hockey: The Effects of Body Checking. Pediatrics, 105 (3), 657-658.

Anger: The Turbulent Emotion (1983). Human Relations Media,Pleasantville, NY.

Baker, J. (2001) Genes and Training for Athletic Performance Revisited. Sportscience, 5(2).

Baker, J., Horton, S., Robertson-Wilson, J. and Wall, M. Nurturing Sport Expertise: Factors Influencing the Development of Elite Athlete. (2003) Journal of Sports Science and Medicine, 2, 1-9.

Baker, J., Yardley, J. and Cote, J. (2003) Coach Behaviors and Athlete Satisfaction in Team and Individual Sports. International Journal of Sport Psychology, 34, 226-239.

Bandura, A. and Walters,R.H. (1963) Social Learning and Personality Development. Holt, Rhinehart and Winston, New York, NY.

Barnett, N. P., Smoll, F.L., and Smith, R.E. (1992) Effects of Enhancing Coach-Athlete Relationships on Youth Sport Attrition. The Sport Psychologist, 6, 111-127.

Beck, R.C. (1978) Motivation: Theories and Principles, Prentice Hall Inc., Englewood Cliffs, NJ.

Bergin, D.A. and Habusta, S.F. (2004) Goal Orientations of Young Male Ice Hockey Players and Their Parents. The Journal of Genetic Psychology, 165(4), 383-397.

Bernstein, D.A.,and Borkovev, T.D. (1973) Progressive Relaxation Training. Research press, Champaign, ILL.

Bouchard, C., Malina, R.M., and Perusse, L. (1997) Genetics of Fitness and Physical Performance. Human Kinetics, Champaign,ILL.

Burley, S.K.,Almo, S.C.,Bonanno,J.B.,Capel, M.,Chance, M.R.,Gaas terland,T.,Lin,D.,Sali,A., Studier, F.W., Swaminathan, S. (1999) Structural Genomics: Beyond The Human Genome Project. Nature Genetics, Vol 23, 151-157.

Butt, D.S. (1987) The Psychology of Sport. The Behavior, Motivation, Personality and Performance of Athletes, Van Nostrand Reinhold, New York.

Canning, P.M., Courage, M.L. and Frizzell, L. (2004) Prevalence of overweight and obesity in a provincial population of Canadian preschool children, Canadian Medical Association Journal, August 3, 171 (3), 240.

Cannon, W.B. (1929) Bodily Changes in Pain, Hunger, Fear and Rage. Appleton-Century, New York, NY.

Cantu, R.C. (1986) Guidelines for Return to Contact Sports After A Cerebral Concussion. Physician and Sports Medicine, 14(10),75-76.

Carey, E. (2006) Study Slams Kids' Bodychecking, The Toronto Star,February, 6, Toronto, ON.

Cassel, R.N. and Stancik, M.A. (1982) The Leadership Ability Evaluation Revised. Western Psychological Services, Los Angeles, CA.

Cattell, R. and Erber, H.W. and Tatsuoka, M.M. (1970) Handbook for the Sixteen Personality Factor Questionnaire. Institute for the Personality Ability Testing, Champaign, ILL.

CBA News (1993) NHL Pension Plan. At http://www.Nnlcba news. com/cba/article21.html

Claverie, J.M. (2001) Gene Number. What If There Are Only 30,000 Human Genes?", Science, 291, 1255-57.

Cox, D. (2007) Its Time for the NHL to Arrest Policemen. March 03,Toronto Star, Toronto, ON.

Cox, D. (2007) Finally A Step Forward: Campbell Justified in Looking At Fights, Toronto Star, March 23, Toronto, ON.

Darley, J. and Latane, B. (1968) Bystander Intervention in Emergencies: Diffusion of Responsibility. Journal of Personality and Social Psychology, 10, 202-214.

Diamond,D.,Bontje,P.,Dinger,R.,Duplacey,J.,Zweig, E.,Paternak, J.,(2003) Total NHL, Published by Dan Diamond and Associates, Toronto, ON.

Dollard, J.,Miller,N.E.,Doob,L.W.,Mowrer, O.H.,Sears, R.R.(1939) Frustration and Aggression.Yale University Press, New Haven, CONN.

Dollard, J.and Miller, N. (1941) Social Learning and Imitation,Yale University Press, New Haven, CONN.

Dorland's Medical Dictionary (1976) Twenty-fifth Edition. WB.Saunders, Toronto, ON.

Drake, D. and Cifu, D. (2006) Repetitive Head Injury Syndrome. emedicine.com (Retrieved January 19, 2007)

Duda, J.L. (1996) Maximizing Motivation in Sport and Physical Education Among Children and Adolescents: The Case of Greater Task Involvement, Quest, 48, 3, 290-302.

Dunn, J.G. and J.C. Dunn (1999) Goal Orientations, Perceptions of Aggression and Sportsmanship in Elite Male Youth Ice Hockey Players. The Sports Psychologist, 13, 183-200.

Eibl-Eibesfeldt, I. (1961) The Fighting Behavior of Animals. Scientific American, 202, 112-122.

Ericsson,K.A.,Krampe,R.T.,Tesch-Romer,C. (1993) The Role of Deliberate Practice in the Acquisition of Expert Performance. Psychological Review, 100, 363-406.

Erikson, E. H. (1963) Childhood and Society. Norton, New York, NY.

Eysenck, H.J. (1967) The Biological Basis of Personality. Thomas Pub., Springfield, Ill.

Eysenck,H.J. (1984) Personal Communication at the XXIII International Congress of Psychology, Acapulco, Mexico.

Freud, S. (1966) The Ego and Mechanisms of Defense. International University Press, New York, NY

Gardner, H. (1983) Frames of Mind: The Theory of Multiple Intelligences, Basic Books, New York, NY.

Gilbert, J., Cruickshank, G and Dudley, R. (2004) The Library Shakespeare, Robert Frederick Limited, Glasgow, SCOT.

Hagel, B.E., Marko,J., Dryden,D., Couperthwaite,A.B., Sommerfeldt,J.,& Rowe,B.H. (2006), Effects of Bodychecking On Injury Rates Among Minor Ice Hockey Players. Canadian Medical Association Journal, 175(2), 155-160.

Hare, R. (1993) Without Conscience, Guilford Press, New York, NY.

Harlow, H.F. (1958) The Nature of Love, American Psychologist, 13, 673-685.

Harmon, K.G. (1999) Assessment and Management of Concussion in Sports. American Family Physician, Vol. 60(3).

Hass, E. T. (1988) Aggression and Violence in Minor Hockey. In Runner, Volume XXVI (4) , 22-24.

Helsen,W.F.,Hodges,N.J.,Van Winckel,J.,Starkes, J.L.(2000) The Roles of Talent, Physical Precocity and Practise in the Development of Soccer Expertise. Journal of Sports Sciences, 18, 727-736.

Helsen,W.F., Starkes,J.& Hodges,N.A.,(1998) Team Sports and the Theory of Deliberate Practice. Journal of Sport and Exercise Psychology, 20, 12-34.

Hockey Canada Officiating Program Standard of Play and Rules Emphasis, 2006-2007, Hockey Canada, WWW.HockeyCanada. Ca

Hockey Trainers Certification Program (1998). Hockey Development Centre Ontario, Participants Manual, Published by Canadian Hockey Association, Gloucester, ON.

Holbrook,J.E. and Barr,J.K. (1997) Contemporary Coaching: Issues and Trends. Cooper Publishing, Carmel, IN.

Hopkins, W.G. (2001) Genes and Training for Athletic Performance. Sportscience 5(1).

Kalchman, L. (2003) Minor Hockey Won't Budge on Bodychecking Policy The Toronto Star, January, 16, Toronto, ON.

Kalchman, L. (2003) Making NHL a Very Long Shot. The Toronto Star,January 28, Toronto, ON.

King, W.J. and LeBlanc, C.M. (2006) Should Body Checking Be Allowed In Minor Hockey, Canadian Medical Association Journal,175 (2), 163-166.

Kolb, B. and Fantie, B. (1989) Development of the Child's Brain and Behavior. In C.R. Reynolds and E. Fletcher-Janzen (Eds.) Handbook of Clinical Child Neuropsychology (pp. 17-39, Plenum, New York, NY.

Latane, B. and Darley, J. (1968) Group Inhibition of Bystander Intervention, Journal of Personality and Social Psychology, 10, 215-221.

Le Clair, J. (1992) Winners and Losers. Sport and Physical Activity in the 90's. Thompson Educational Publishing, Inc.,Toronto, ON.

Lockwood, K.L. & Brophey, P. (2004) The Effect of a Plyometrics Program Intervention on Skating Speed in Junior Hockey Players. The Sport Journal, Vol 7, (3), Summer/Fall.

Lorenz, K. (1963) On Aggression. Harcourt, Brace and World. New York, NY.

MacGregor, R. (2007) This Country: Pleas for Reason Ignored as Hockey Violence Rears its Ugly Head Again. February 26, The Globe and Mail, Toronto, ON.

MacGregor, R. (2007) This Country: Give Your Head A Shake If You Don't Think its Time to Knock Out the Fighting, March 26, The Globe and Mail, Toronto, ON.

MacGregor, R. (2007) This Country: NHL Lacks Brains for Tolerating Hits to the Head, April 16, The Globe and Mail, Toronto, ON.

McKelvie, S.J., Valliant, P.M., and Asu, M.E., (1985). Physical Training and Personality Factors as Predictors of Marathon Time and Training Injury. Perceptual and Motor Skills, 60, 551-560.

Millon, T. (1981) Disorders of Personality:DSM-III, Wiley, New York, NY.

Miller, N. (1959) Liberalization of Basic S-R Concepts: Extensions to Conflict Behavior, Motivation and Social Learning. In S.Koch (Ed.) Psychology: A Study of Science, Vol. 2, McGraw Hill, New York, NY.

Miller, S. (2001) The Complete Player: The Psychology of Winning Hockey, Stoddart, Toronto, ON.

Nack, W. and Munson, L. Out of Control, SportsIllustrated, Flashback,http://sportsillustrated. cnn.com/features/cover/news/2000/12/08yir_ courtroom2/

Nomellini, S., and Katz, R.C. (1983) Effects of Anger Control Training on Abusive Parents. Cognitive Therapy and Research, 7(1), 57-68.

Novaco, R.W. (1976) The Functions and Regulation of the Arousal of Anger. American Journal of Psychiatry, 133, 1124-1128.

Novaco, R.W. (1979) The Cognitive Regulation of Anger and Stress. Cognitive Behavioral Intervention: Theory, Research and Procedures. Academic Press, New York, NY.

Parcels, J. (2002) Chances of Making it in Pro Hockey. Downloaded from the Cumberland Minor Hockey Association Web Site: WWW:cumberland minorhockey.ca

Pavlov, I. (1927) Conditioned Reflexes. Oxford University Press,Oxford, ENG.

Pennisi, E. (2003) A Low Number Wins the GeneSweep Pool. Science,300, 1484.

Piaget, J. (1947) The Psychology of Intelligence. Keagan Paul Pub., London, ENG.

Revelle, W. (1993) Individual Differences in Personality and Motivation: Non-cognitive determinants of Cognitive Performance in A. Braddeley and L. Weiskrantz (eds) Attention, Selection, Awareness and Control: A Tribute to Donald Broadbent. Pgs 346 -373, Oxford University Press, Oxford, ENG.

Ryan, H. Trial Report; No Leniency: Junta Gets 6 to 10 Years. CourtTVNews, WWW.courttv.com/trials/ junta/012502_ctv. html

Segalowitz, S.J. and Davies, P.L. (2004) Charting the Maturation of the Frontal Lobe: An Electrophysiological Strategy. Brain and Cognition, 55, 116-133.

Shreeve, James (2006) Genetic Trails Left by our Ancestors are Leading Scientists back Across Time an Epic Discovery of Human Migration. National Geographic Vol. 209 (3), 60—73.

Skinner, B.F. (1971) Beyond Freedom and Dignity, Alfred A. Knopf, New York, NY.

Smith, M.D. (1979) Towards an Explanation of Hockey Violence. Canadian Journal of Sociology, 4, 105-124.

Starkes, J.L. (2000) The Road to Expertise. Is Practice the Only Determinant? International Journal of Sport Psychology, 31, 431-451.

Stewart, C. and Meyers, M. (2004) Motivational Traits of Elite Young Players. Physical Educator, Vol. 61 (4), 213-219.

Stuss, D.T. (1992) Biological and Psychological Development of Executive Functions, Brain and Cognition, 20(1), 8-23.

Terry, P.C. and Howe, B.L. (1984) Coaching Preferences of Athletes. Canadian Journal of Applied Sport Science, 9, 201-208.

Tremblay, M.S., and Willms, J.D. (2001) Secular Trends in the Body Mass Index of Canadian School Children, Canadian Medical Association Journal, 164(7), 970.

Tresniowski,A.,Duffy,T.,Driscoll,A.,Ehrich,K.,Rozsa,L., Ellman,S.,Harmel,K.,Stockler,B.,Ballard, M., Wescott,G.,and Wilstach,N.(2002). A Moment's Fatal Fury, People, Jan.28, 57 (3), Pp. 50.

Trudel,P.,Cote,J.,and Sylvestre,F.(1996) Systematic Observation of Ice Hockey Referees During Games. Journal of Sport Behavior, Vol. 19., Issue 1

Vallance, J.K., Dunn, J.G. and Causgrove Dunn, J.L. (2006). Perfectionism, Anger and Situation Criticality in Competitive Youth Ice Hockey. Journal of Sport and Exercise Psychology, 28, 383-406.

Valliant,P.M.,Simpson-Housely,P.,and McKelvie, S.J. (1981) Personality in Athletic and Non-athletic College Groups. Perceptual and Motor Skills, 1981, 963-966.

Valliant, P.M. (1981) Personality and Injury in Competitive Runners, Perceptual and Motor Skills, 53, 251-253.

Valliant, P.M. (1981) Do Marathoners Differ from Joggers in Personality Profile. The Journal of Sports Medicine and Physical Fitness, 21 (1), 62-69.

Valliant, P.M. (1980) Injury and Personality Traits in Non-competitive Runners. The Journal of Sports Medicine and Physical Fitness, 341-346.

Valliant, P.M. and Asu, M. E. (1985) Exercise and Its Effect on Cognition and Physiology in Older Adults. Perceptual and Motor Skills, 61, 1235-1241.

Watson, J.B. (1930) Behaviorism. University of Chicago Press,Chicago, ILL.

Wuerth, S., Lee, M.J., and Alfermann, D. (2004) Parental Involvement and Athletes Career in Youth Sport. Psychology of Sport and Exercise, 5, 21-33.

Xiang, H., Smith, G.A. and Hostetler, S. (2005) Characteristics of Ice Hockey-Related Injuries Treated in US Emergency

Department, 2001-2003: In Reply (2005), Pediatrics, 115 (5),1449.

Zimbardo, P.G. (1970) The Human Choice: Individuation, Reason and Order Versus Deindividuation, Impulse and Chaos. In W.J. Arnold and D. Levine (Eds), Nebraska Symposium on Motivation, pp 237-307. University of Nebraska Press, Lincoln, NB.

HOCKEY PLAYER SELF EVALUATION

NOTE: RATE YOURSELF ON EACH OF THE FOLLOWING STATEMENTS.

1) DESIRE TO WIN
(1) BELOW AVERAGE (2) AVERAGE (3) ABOVE AVERAGE

2) PASSING/CARRYING/SHOOTING THE PUCK
(1) BELOW AVERAGE (2) AVERAGE (3) ABOVE AVERAGE

3) SKATING/RUSHING/BACK-CHECKING
(1) BELOW AVERAGE (2) AVERAGE (3) ABOVE AVERAGE

4) BODY CHECKING/STOPPING OPPONENT
(1) BELOW AVERAGE (2) AVERAGE (3) ABOVE AVERAGE

MY STRENGTHS DURING THE GAME:

_____

_____

_____

_____

_____

THINGS I NEED TO CHANGE SO MY TEAM CAN WIN THE GAMES:

_____

_____

_____

_____

_____

MY OVERALL RATING:

(Poor 1 2 3 4 5 6 7 8 9 10 11 12 Excellent)

GOALIE SELF EVALUATION

NOTE: RATE YOURSELF ON EACH OF THE FOLLOWING STATEMENTS.

1) DESIRE TO WIN
(1) BELOW AVERAGE (2) AVERAGE (3) ABOVE AVERAGE

2) STOPPING THE PUCK/QUICK REFLEXES
(1) BELOW AVERAGE (2) AVERAGE (3) ABOVE AVERAGE

3) PUSHING THE HOCKEY PLAYER OUT OF MY GOALIE CREASE
(1) BELOW AVERAGE (2) AVERAGE (3) ABOVE AVERAGE

4) SHOTS ON GOAL/ SAVES /SCORES AGAINST
(1) BELOW AVERAGE (2) AVERAGE (3) ABOVE AVERAGE

MY STRENGTHS DURING THE GAME/PRACTICE:
_____
_____
_____
_____

THINGS I NEED TO CHANGE SO THAT MY TEAM CAN WIN THE GAME:

_____

_____

_____

_____

_____

MY OVERALL RATING:

(Poor 1 2 3 4 5 6 7 8 9 10 11 12 Excellent)

APPENDIX 3

STRESS AND ANGER MANAGEMENT

A. INTRODUCTION TO STRESS AND ANGER MANAGEMENT

Stress was first defined by Hans Selye as one of the major problems of the twentieth century. As we approach the twenty first century, stress will become more problematic and create emotionally volatile reactions. Human beings are constantly vigilant about stressors in the environment because it would seem that these create tension and cause anger to rise to the surface. Anger that is channelled into positive energy allows one to work diligently and exercise harder. At times however anger becomes excessive and is turned inward leading to physical maladies and depression. At other times it is directed outward and expressed as aggression and violence toward others. In these situations anger can become a dangerous emotion and will consume one with its energy. The high incidence of verbal hostility, threatening and road rage are only a few instances of anger that becomes displaced. This volatile emotion can cause one to lose control of their behaviour.

When anger becomes excessive in hockey parents, it leads to a loss of control. The verbal profanities, emotional abuse of players, coaches and officials are only a few of the instances of anger that is out of control at the arena. At times it can lead to mob violence and occasionally it can lead to the death of someone who happens to be in the wrong place at the wrong time. Anger can be useful as an energizer but at times can spew its venomous rage. Anger externalized is one of the gravest forms of evil. When anger becomes directed at those believed to be the root of their problems it can cause harmful and long lasting effects. When aggression arises, it can be released with violence and hostile attacks.

It is in a hockey parent's best interests to understand the emotion of anger which is often triggered by stressors. These external stimuli create emotional volatility and allow for the expression of aggression and rage. I have included some information below so that the reader can gain some insight into the basics of an Anger Management Program. With this information one can begin to understand how stress leads to anger which if not channelled properly only leads to aggression. The following information will provide the reader with a starting point. For those parents who believe they could use some instruction in this area, this could be sought out by attending "Emotion Control Programs" that are offered by agencies in most communities.

THE ANGER MANAGEMENT PROGRAM:

WHAT IS A STRESSOR?
This is stimulus (situation or person) that creates a feeling of anxiety or pressure. You become upset and tense when this stimulus is in your presence.
Examples:

1. Situation/Event = A tense hockey game
2. Person(s) = A hockey parent screaming obscenities at the referee

WHAT IS STRESS?

The body's internal response to the situation or person. The person becomes tense, upset, blood pressure rises and your heart pounds.

ABC'S OF STRESS AND ANGER.

A=   Antecedent   (Stressor)
B=   Behaviour   (Body Arousal)
C=   Consequence   (Reaction)

A STRESSOR Situation/Person	B BODY AROUSAL Underlying Change	C REACTION Emotion in Biochemistry

Example:(1)

Pressured Game	Agitation	Fear/Anger/Rage

When you are at practises or games certain situations/events or person(s) can cause upset. When these incidents occur the hockey parent/spectator becomes aroused (anxious/tense). This leads to a number of reactions. One's ability to inhibit these feelings will have an impact on their reactions. The parent who can't control these emotions, responds with fear, anger or rage. The reaction is dependent on a number of influential factors including one's thoughts (cognition), personality and/or state of mind. External factors including prior substance use (ie. alcohol/drugs) can influence your reactions.

EFFECT OF STRESSORS:

Stressors cause a person to react. The Individual must identify the stressors that affect their underlying emotions. The hockey parent must either attempt to avoid these situations/people or control the underlying upset they experience when they are exposed to these situations or in contact with these people. The reaction that you experience internally creates the tension. This could lead to an emotionally charged reaction (ie. anger).

1) BODY AROUSAL:
Stressors cause the brain's emotional centre (hypothalamus) to get charged up. The hypothalamus in turn sends messages to the body via the nervous system. Internal chemical messengers are released: (Catecholamines and Cortisone)

Catecholamines are released immediately from the adrenal glands. These cause your heart to pump rapidly and blood pressure rises. This underlying activity makes you tense and anxious. This response makes you alert and puts you in a state of readiness so that you can react to the stimulus (stressor).

Cortisone is a chemical also released from the adrenal glands. The cortisone takes over the job of maintaining the body in a state of readiness once the catecholamines have been depleted.

2) REACTION:
The reaction of the stressed hockey parent will depend on their perception of the event. If one is able to cope with the agitation created by stressful events, this will allow the person to return to a neutral state and the tension in the body will decrease. Some parents are not able to cope with the agitation. These individuals may become highly anxious and experience upset; others will become emotionally charged by the event. This could lead the parent to internalize their anger and become depressed; a release of the emotion would be expressed in reactions including aggression, hostility.

Examples of Negative Reactions:

a) Reacting to the Situation—becoming angry at the event that has precipitated your emotional reaction by yelling emotionally charged comments or using profanities (swearing) or negative expletives (ie. you idiot)

b) Violence against Others—attacking the individual who created the stress (ie. punching out another parent; attacking the referee).

c) Depression—feeling a sense of despondency when others (ie. coaches, parents or officials don't value you or your child's performance on the ice).

3) RESOLVING UPSET THROUGH ANGER MANAGEMENT:
The best way for the hockey parent to cope with stress and the resulting emotion of anger is to seek ways of removing oneself from the situation; a second way would be to learn some techniques that will reduce the level of arousal in the brain and body.

By knowing ones level of emotionality (ie. reaction to a stressor that creates emotional upset) will allow the parent to recognize their signs/symptoms of anger. These signs could include the following: tension in the muscles, elevated heat in the body (ie. face, ears), anxiety or a personal feeling of loss of control (ie. urge to hit someone).

The parent can attempt to undertake a number of positive actions if they feel tense, pressured, anxious or angry. These could include the following:

1) Leaving the situation that created stress. Go for a walk or a jog and return to the event (ie. hockey game) when you feel relaxed. This approach is useful because responding in this manner allows your body to use up/burn the excess biochemi-

cals (ie. catecholamines and cortisol) that are being released into your body and creating the agitation and upset.

2) Attempting to control the biochemical and emotional energy caused by stress through relaxation techniques including deep breathing and relaxation training. These include the methods of D. Bernstein and T. Borkovec (Progressive Relaxation Training) or R. Novaco (Anger Management); these are cited in the references. If you find yourself extremely upset go to your vehicle and practise these exercises.

3) Creating a relaxed mental/emotional state by imaging positive experiences (ie.lying on a beach) and combining these images with progressive relaxation methods. During these sessions you experience the deep feelings of contentment and relaxation.

4) Purchase some tapes on relaxation training and anger management and listen to these often when you are at home or in your car. Once you have the skills you will be able to engage in this exercise with little effort.

INDEX

ISBN 1425133335-5

9 781425 133351